THE PRINCIPAL AS

Professional Learning Community Leader

Introduction to the *Leading Student Achievement* Series

The *Leading Student Achievement* series is a joint publication of the Ontario Principals' Council (OPC) and Corwin Press as part of an active commitment to support and develop excellent school leadership. One of the roles of OPC is to identify, design, develop, and deliver workshops that meet the learning needs of school leaders. Most of the handbooks in this series were originally developed as one-day workshops by their authors to share their expertise in key areas of school leadership. Following are the five handbooks in this series:

The Principal as Professional Learning Community Leader

The Principal as Data-Driven Leader

The Principal as Early Literacy Leader

The Principal as Instructional Leader in Literacy

The Principal as Mathematics Leader

Each handbook in the *Leading Student Achievement* series is grounded in action and is designed as a hands-on, practical guide to support school leaders in their roles as instructional leaders. From novice principals who are assuming the principalship to experienced principals who are committed to continuous learning, readers from all levels of experience will benefit from the accessible blend of theory and practice presented in these handbooks. The provision of practical strategies that principals can use immediately in their schools makes this series a valuable resource to all who are committed to improving student achievement.

THE PRINCIPAL AS

Professional Learning Community Leader

LEADING STUDENT ACHIEVEMENT
SERIES

A Joint Publication

For information:

Corwin Press
A SAGE Company
2455 Teller Road
Thousand Oaks, California 91320
www.corwinpress.com

SAGE India Pvt. Ltd.
B 1/I 1 Mohan Cooperative
  Industrial Area
Mathura Road, New Delhi 110 044
India

SAGE Ltd.
1 Oliver's Yard
55 City Road
London EC1Y 1SP
United Kingdom

SAGE Asia-Pacific Pte. Ltd.
33 Pekin Street #02-01
Far East Square
Singapore 048763

Printed in the United States of America.

Library of Congress Cataloging-in-Publication Data

The principal as professional learning community leader/Ontario Principals' Council.
    p. cm.
"A joint publication with Ontario Principals' Council."
Includes bibliographical references.
ISBN 978-1-4129-6313-8 (cloth)
ISBN 978-1-4129-6314-5 (pbk.)
    1. School principals—Professional relationships. 2. Educational leadership.
I. Ontario Principals' Council.

LB2831.9.P748 2009
371.2′012—dc22   2008035245

This book is printed on acid-free paper.

08   09   10   11   12   10   9   8   7   6   5   4   3   2   1

Acquisitions Editor:	Debra Stollenwerk
Editorial Assistant:	Allison Scott
Developmental Editor:	Daniel J. Richcreek
Production Editor:	Libby Larson
Copy Editor:	Paula L. Fleming
Typesetter:	C&M Digitals (P) Ltd.
Proofreader:	Theresa Kay
Indexer:	Terri Corry
Cover Designer:	Lisa Riley

Contents

Acknowledgments

The Ontario Principals' Council gratefully acknowledges Linda Massey, the author of *The Principal as Professional Learning Community Leader*.

Linda Massey is a consultant for Education Leadership Canada, the professional development division of the Ontario Principals' Council. Before her retirement from the Peel District School Board, Ontario, Canada, in 2003, Linda's lifelong interest in professional development led her to develop and present many professional learning opportunities to her colleagues within her school district and throughout the province of Ontario, including local and international workshops and conferences. Linda's involvement with OPC began as a practicing administrator and, since 1999, has included workshops for principals and vice principals throughout Ontario titled *Elementary and Secondary School Evaluation Policies in the New Curriculum, Implementing Secondary School Curriculum Reform*, and *Principal Action Research and Professional Learning Communities: The Principal as Instructional Leader.* As an education consultant since 2003, Linda continues to develop workshops, organize professional learning opportunities for school leaders, write resource materials, and coordinate projects for the Ontario Principals' Council.

The Ontario Principals' Council also wishes to gratefully acknowledge the contributions of the designers and deliverers of the original *Professional Learning Communities: The Principal as Instructional Leader* workshop: Joanne Grozelle, Cindy Harris, Linda Massey, Steve McCombe, and Brian Serafini. As well, the efforts of Ethne Cullen and Linda Massey of the Ontario Principals' Council in coordinating this joint OPC/Corwin project are gratefully acknowledged.

Corwin Press gratefully acknowledges the contributions of the following reviewers:

Jeffrey M. Cornejo, EdD
Principal
Robert A. Millikan Senior High School
Long Beach, CA

Lois Brown Easton
Coach and Consultant
LBE Learning
Boulder, CO

Dr. Daniel C. Elliott
Professor, Curriculum Specialist
Azusa Pacific University
Azusa, CA

Arthur Foresta
Leadership Development Facilitator
New Visions for Public Schools
New York, NY

Dr. Erika L. Hunt
Project Director, Illinois State Action
    for Education Leadership Project
Illinois State University
Normal, IL

Barry W. Knight
Principal
Palmetto Middle School
Williamston, SC

Primus M. Moore
Assistant Principal/School Site Support Coordinator
McAlester Public Schools
McAlester, OK

Introduction

The Principal as Professional Learning Community Leader is designed to provide principals with hands-on, practical support as they build professional learning communities (PLCs) in their schools. Creating a collaborative culture for action that focuses on improving student achievement is a complex undertaking. Principals need to understand why PLCs provide an effective infrastructure for continuous school improvement. This book provides a convincing rationale for developing the attributes of a PLC that principals can share with their teachers to begin the work of transforming instructional and leadership practice in their schools. And this book supports principals in their role as instructional leaders. A variety of strategies are presented to principals that can be used when introducing the concept of PLCs to staff. These strategies are outlined step-by-step in several Professional Development Modules at the back of the book, which school leaders can use with teachers to do the following:

- Lay the foundations of mission, vision, values, and goals
- Build the pillars of collaborative teamwork, teacher capacity, leadership capacity, and professional development that support teacher learning teams
- Raise the roof of continuous learning and improvement
- Celebrate PLC accomplishments

This handbook offers principals valuable tools, templates, and techniques on how to start building a PLC in a school that can be easily adapted to any particular school context.

Audience

Administrators with a wide variety of experience will find this handbook helpful. Novice principals will find step-by-step plans and practical strategies to use with staff to create the conditions within which PLCs thrive. Principals assuming the role of PLC leader because of their conviction of its value in improving schools can use this handbook as a planning and delivery tool in their goal to develop PLCs in their schools. Experienced principals will find that the book provides a valuable review of PLC knowledge and supplies some new tools that support and sustain PLCs.

Handbook Organization

Building a PLC takes time, expertise, and effort. This handbook is designed to save time by providing principals with ready-made planning templates and professional development modules that they can use with their teachers. A summary of current research about PLCs helps principals to understand the key attributes of PLCs themselves and, more importantly, how to share this knowledge with staff. Much of this handbook is modeled around a graphic organizer, the PLC Edifice, used as an analogy for the construction of a PLC, which will make the stages of developing a PLC clearly evident to you and to staff.

Chapter 1 provides the rationale for building PLCs in schools. It introduces the attributes of a PLC in the form of an edifice, a grand structure, which visually presents the foundations, pillars, and sustaining roof of the analogy that provides a framework for understanding the actions needed to establish a PLC in a school.

Chapter 2 outlines the role of principals in leading a PLC. Of special interest is an explanation of the leadership practices that current research says have the most impact on school improvement: setting directions, developing people, redesigning the organization, and managing the instructional program (Leithwood, Day, Sammons, Harris, & Hopkins, 2006). This leadership model is applied to the construction of a PLC in a school.

Chapter 3 provides principals with the tools for planning the start-up of a PLC. Principals learn how to set up a PLC Steering Team of school leaders, how to use a PLC Snapshot Assessment as a diagnostic tool, and how to create a PLC Portfolio to track the school's progress in becoming a PLC. The PLC Learning Grid, a reflection and planning template, is introduced at the end of this chapter.

Chapter 4 explains the importance of developing a mission, vision, values, and goals statements as the foundation of a PLC. This chapter introduces two Professional Development Modules (found at the back of the book in the Principal's Toolkit), which principals can use at staff meetings to develop these statements. Detailed instructions and templates are provided to facilitate this step. A set of guiding questions that principals can ask themselves about the process and a PLC Learning Grid are provided at the end of the chapter.

Chapter 5 focuses on how to create the teacher learning teams that are essential to a PLC. The four pillars of collaborative teamwork, teacher capacity, leadership capacity, and professional development are explained. The third Professional Development Module (found at the back of the book) is introduced here for principals to use with staff when introducing learning teams. Guiding questions and a PLC Learning Grid are also provided.

Chapter 6 looks ahead in the PLC process to consider the necessity of building in a process that allows for the continuous learning and improvement that is an essential attribute of a PLC. The Reflection and Action graphic shows the series of steps that the PLC Principal uses to sustain the energy of continuous school improvement in an ongoing cycle. Finally, a variety of ways to celebrate the accomplishments of the school as a PLC is shared.

The Principal's Toolkit

The Principal's Toolkit at the back of the book provides a variety of strategies for administrators through Professional Development Modules, Case Studies, and Reproducibles to support the effort of initiating a collaborative culture for improving student achievement.

Professional Development Modules guide administrators through professional development sessions where principals, teacher leadership teams, and teachers work collaboratively in one-day workshops, half-day training sessions, or one-hour portions of staff meetings devoted to staff development.

Case Studies are detailed examples written by principals who have worked in their schools to create PLCs. Four of these case studies describe how principals set up PLCs in their schools. These case studies are useful resources for the jigsaw activity to develop learning teams in the first PD Module. The fifth case study supports Chapter 2 on leadership practices of a PLC principal by providing the rationale and a proposal template for establishing a principal/vice principal learning team in a school district.

Reproducibles provide administrators and leadership teams with easy-to-copy, full-page versions of the graphic organizers and templates used in the Professional Development Modules and throughout the text.

CHAPTER 1

Building Professional Learning Communities

A professional learning community (PLC) is about the synergy of collaborative action. The term *synergy* is derived from the Greek word *synergos*, meaning "working together," and describes instances where increased effectiveness and achievement are produced by combined action. Improved student achievement is one instance where research has demonstrated that educators who work collaboratively produce an effect on student results that is greater than the sum of individual teacher effort (Fullan, 2005c). Effective PLCs provide the conditions necessary for the synergy that drives school improvement. Students, teachers, and school leaders are the recipients of the powerful effects of collaborative action as practiced in professional learning communities.

Professional learning communities have become a significant field for research in the past 15 years, as researchers and practitioners in schools explore the effectiveness of schools that have embraced the principles of professional learning communities. In educational literature, *professional learning community* has come to mean a school environment where teachers work collaboratively in purposefully designed groups to improve student achievement within a structure of support provided by the school administrator. In such schools, principals create a culture where teachers work actively in teams with the shared purpose of producing successful learning outcomes for all students. Stoll and Seashore Louis (2007) describe a PLC as a school where the focus is on "(1) professional learning; (2) within the context of a cohesive group; (3) that focuses on collective knowledge, and (4) occurs within an ethic of interpersonal caring that permeates the life of teachers, students and school leaders" (p. 3).

This research has prompted many educators to explore the efficacy of professional learning communities as a strategy to increase student learning and achievement. What educators find is that PLCs provide a school learning environment that supports improvement of leadership and teacher capacity. By developing the collective ability to act together to bring about change, PLCs have proven to be very supportive of school improvement. When principals, vice principals, teacher leaders, and teachers work together to begin the process of building professional learning communities within their schools, they are making a profound commitment to build capacity. By working collaboratively, educators develop new skills, explore and utilize enhanced instructional resources, and grow in shared commitment and motivation to improve student achievement (Fullan, 2005c).

This book provides principals who are starting to build PLCs in their schools with a number of practical strategies that have proven effective in building a culture of collaborative action for school improvement. Within this handbook, school leaders can choose from a variety of strategies: graphic organizers, professional development modules with workshop guides, assessment and tracking templates, note-taking charts, staff memos, and case studies. These strategies support the PLC leader in setting directions, building relationships, developing people, redesigning the organization, and managing the instructional program—the core practices of successful school leaders (Leithwood, Day, Sammons, Harris, & Hopkins, 2006).

WHY PROFESSIONAL LEARNING COMMUNITIES?

Professional learning communities are an instrument for facilitating enhanced learning, teaching, and leadership capacity at all levels of the education system. When educational leaders become determined and purposeful about improving student learning, they seek first to agree on the means to this end. The means, or pathway, as the literature under study suggests, is professional learning communities.

The study of PLCs is led by educational leaders such as Alan Blankstein, Paul Bredeson, Rebecca DuFour, Richard DuFour, Robert Eaker, Michael Fullan, Andy Hargreaves, Larry Lazotte, Mike Schmoker, Karen Seashore Louis, Peter Senge, Richard Stiggins, and Louise Stoll. Compelling research supports the value of professional learning communities. These prominent members of the school improvement research community endorse the implementation of PLCs as a significant means of building student, teacher, school leader, and system capacity.

There is a strong rationale for the continued development of the attributes of learning communities in our schools and the greater educational community. Prominent researchers advocate for the efficacy of PLCs because their findings provide evidence that student achievement is influenced by the development of a collaborative action process that focuses on improved student learning. A number of studies provide evidence that the operation of purposeful interaction characterizes successful schools (Fullan, 2001). Researchers conclude that a structure for greater collaboration among teachers that is implemented properly and sustained over time results in a strong professional community that, in turn, contributes to improved student learning.

Teacher collaboration that is evidence based improves the quality of instructional practice, resulting in significant, measurable improvements in student learning (Hargreaves, 2003; Schmoker, 2005). As a result of findings like these, the National Staff Development Council recognizes the importance of learning communities in its *Standards for Staff Development* (2001), where the first of 12 standards supports the implementation of "Learning Communities: Staff development that improves the learning of all students: organizes adults into learning communities where goals are aligned with those of the school and district" ("Learning Communities: The Standard").

A review of PLC literature points to seven key attributes of effective professional learning communities:

1. Student learning

2. Shared purpose

3. Collaborative teamwork

4. Teacher capacity

5. Leadership capacity

6. Professional development

7. Continuous learning

This chapter examines these seven attributes of professional learning communities within the context of a graphic organizer, the PLC Edifice. This serves as an analogy to present the concepts that researchers and practitioners consider most characteristic of effective professional learning communities. This approach is designed to support principals and their faculties in the implementation of strategies that promote effective PLCs, addressing the needs of students, teachers, and leaders within their schools.

THE PLC EDIFICE: AN ANALOGY

School leaders and teachers assume the roles of architect, building contractor, co-owner, and renovator as they create a professional learning community in their schools. Figure 1.1 represents the planning, building, inhabitation, renovation, and enjoyment of a professional learning community. School leaders and teachers begin their work as they collaboratively plan and create the foundation of their PLC with the shared purpose of improving student learning. They can then construct the four pillars of collaborative teamwork, teacher capacity, leadership capacity, and professional development to support the school's learning teams. Finally, the PLC Edifice is capped with a commitment to continuous learning and

Figure 1.1 The PLC Edifice

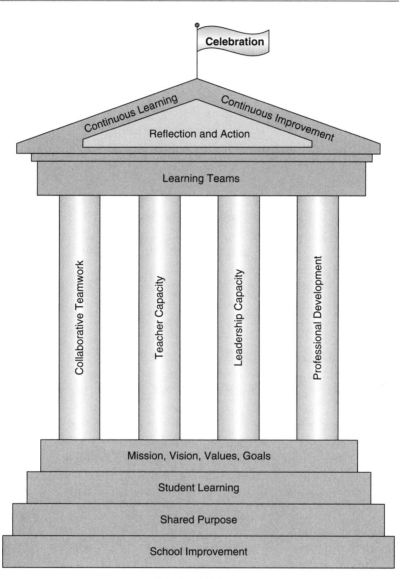

PLC Edifice

improvement, which includes reflection and action. The flag of celebration completes the metaphorical building process.

The Foundations of a PLC

Two PLC attributes, *student learning* and *shared purpose,* serve to focus the attention of educators on school improvement. In effect, these attributes become critical tools for implementers of professional learning communities to capture the imagination and keep it focused on the tasks at hand. Since distractions can sidetrack the effort, implementation of a professional learning community must start with an exercise to build a solid foundation for school improvement. How best to create a blueprint that underpins the planned construction of a professional learning community? One way is to develop the mission, vision, values, and goals of a school (DuFour & Eaker, 1998). Throughout this process, school leaders rely on strong communication skills to build the collaborative culture that supports the construction of their learning community.

Student Learning

Student learning and the commitment to improved student achievement is the first and most essential attribute of professional learning communities. Each of the PLC advocates places student learning and achievement as the foundation of their work on school improvement. It's not enough to ensure that students are taught. The issue is whether they learn. Teachers must ensure that students become ongoing learners with the knowledge, skills, and dispositions that make success possible (DuFour, Eaker, & DuFour, 2005). Blankstein's latest book reflects this theme in its title: *Failure is NOT an Option: Six Principles That Guide Student Achievement in High-Performing Schools* (2004). Our moral purpose as educators is to raise the bar on student learning and close the gap in student achievement (Fullan, 2005b). Results that demonstrate that PLCs make a difference to student learning are an important motivator of continuing research in this area.

Shared Purpose

Shared purpose is the second attribute of professional learning communities. The key word is *shared.* A PLC has a school culture where mission, vision, values, and goals are supportive of student learning through the application of the principles of a professional learning community. Senge (2000) writes convincingly of the discipline of shared vision and mutual purpose in learning communities. Developing a clear and focused mission is one of the building blocks of a professional learning community (Bredeson, 2003). DuFour and Eaker (1998) have written how-to books on developing mission, vision, values, and goals. Essentially, the commitment of school leaders to the principles of professional learning communities and their skills in inspiring their schools to espouse those attributes is of extreme importance to the success of professional learning communities. Principals use words such as *commitment* and *responsibility* to describe the shared purpose of their leadership in building school capacity to impact positively on student learning and achievement.

The Pillars of a PLC

Once the foundations of the professional learning community are firmly in place, it is time to move to the erection of the four critical pillars of the PLC edifice. The pillars of *collaborative teamwork, teacher capacity, leadership capacity,* and *professional development* support the most significant element of a PLC structure: effective teacher learning teams.

Collaborative Teamwork

Collaborative teamwork, according to the literature, is the most significant attribute of professional learning communities. Teachers work together collaboratively in schools in a variety of permutations, such as learning teams, whole-faculty study groups, grade or division teams in elementary schools, and department teams in secondary schools.

Research studies consistently report that collective teacher and leader inquiry results in improved instructional practice, which has a positive influence on student achievement. A PLC is characterized by teams of teachers working with their principals and other school staff to create an environment where problem solving, innovation, reflection on practice, and collaborative professional development to design and implement effective instructional program is the norm (Eason-Watkins, 2005).

To create a school culture based on collaborative inquiry, it is essential to generate the synergy that occurs when the teamwork of a group is working so well that the group's efforts produce the maximum results from the available resources (Lick, 2005). These positive results also contribute to the synergy of teacher collective efficacy, the group's belief in their ability to improve student achievement. When teacher learning teams create the results that the members have worked hard to achieve, professional morale is strengthened.

Successful collaborative teamwork that results in improved student, teacher, and leadership capacity is the most significant attribute of professional learning communities.

Teacher Capacity

The focus on building student capacity for learning is accompanied by the recognition that you can't have better student achievement without working on teacher capacity, the fourth attribute. Working in collaborative teams produces job-embedded professional development. NSDC's *Standards for Staff Development* (2001) insists that "the most powerful forms of staff development occur in ongoing teams that meet on a regular basis . . . for the purposes of learning, joint lesson planning, and problem solving" ("Learning Communities: The Rationale"). The PLC principal strongly supports the growth of teacher instructional expertise.

Research has shown that a positive contributor to improved student achievement is the development of the capacity of teachers to collaborate as they initiate and assess effective instructional practices. Bredeson's (2003) building blocks of a professional learning community include a strong professional culture with an instructional program supported by professional development. Since PLC advocates are lifelong learners themselves, it's not surprising to read their often passionate call to educators at all levels to support the growth of teacher capacity.

Leadership Capacity

The fifth attribute, leadership capacity, recognizes the importance of strong leadership when building a PLC. PLC advocates have written extensively on the role of the leader in creating and sustaining professional learning communities. Since the quality of the leadership of principals and teachers directly impacts the quality of teaching, learning, and relationships in PLCs, "creating, developing and sustaining a professional learning community is a major leadership and management task, one which emerged from the data as a critical strategic process" (Bolam, McMahon, Stoll, Thomas, & Wallace, 2005, p. 117).

Transforming a school into a PLC can only happen when the principal is an advocate for collaborative action and actively supports the faculty's development as a PLC. Principals who exhibit the qualities of a lifelong learner, intellectually engaging themselves in learning experiences and celebrating their personal professional growth, provide a model that inspires their faculties to do the same (Barth, 2005; Hord, 1997).

Principals who work with their learning teams in a collaborative manner build trust and facilitate the positive experiences of increased teacher and leader learning. Leadership capacity within the school grows, and future school and district leaders are nurtured in professional learning communities.

Professional Development

Closely tied to building teacher and leader capacity is the sixth attribute—professional development. This attribute is considered very important to the functioning of effective PLCs. Both administrators and teachers must engage their creative and reflective capacities as learners to strengthen their practice (Bredeson, 2003). Professional development that supports the improvement of the instructional program of the school is an essential pillar of a professional learning community.

A PLC utilizes two types of professional development. Capacity building includes both professional development external to the school and the internal learning that occurs in collaborative teacher teams. PLCs make active use of job-embedded learning, judiciously accessing external professional development when it meets their learning goals. Teachers best develop their instructional practice when they learn by doing and have a process in place to assess the results of their practice and respond to the data. When professional development is continuous, shared, and closely connected to teaching and learning, teacher capacity grows. The collaborative interaction possible in learning teams allows teachers to benefit from the insights of their colleagues (Hargreaves, 2003; Stiggins, 2005). Research has shown that this job-embedded professional development offers that best source of improved teacher capacity.

The Roof of a PLC

Without the seventh attribute of continuous learning, the PLC structure is susceptible to erosion and decay. To stretch the point further, any gains made in constructing an effective professional learning community can be lost unless the PLC is protected from the elements that challenge change in any institution. A professional learning community is sustained by a cyclical process that insists on reflection and action for continuous improvement. Just as a roof shelters a building from the elements, a commitment to continuous learning and improvement supports a school as it addresses the myriad issues that impact improving student achievement.

Continuous Learning

When schools are committed to collaborative teamwork in the service of improving student achievement, continuous learning is a natural development. This seventh attribute of professional learning communities is characterized by a focus on results that supports the ongoing cycle of learning teams as they set goals, take action, review their results, and respond with new goals and further actions to support their own and their students' learning (Hully & Dier, 2005).

An expectation that all teachers and leaders in schools should continue to build their capacities is pervasive in the literature on professional learning communities. However, a focus on continuous learning over time is not easy. It is hard work to sustain the professional learning community model, since learning team members must feel accountable for student achievement results and use these results to fuel continuous improvement (DuFour, Eaker, & DuFour, 2005). Continuous improvement requires continuous reflection and a commitment to take action as a result.

Barth (2005) feels that "there is no more difficult and important job for the educator than to change the prevailing culture of a school so that it will become hospitable to learning," and asks the wonderful question, "Would it not be astonishing if lifelong learning became the 'standard' against which schools, school professionals, and students were evaluated" (p. 132).

Reflection and Action Template

Start the planning process for building a professional learning community in the school by reflecting on your reading about PLCs in Chapter 1. Jot down your initial thoughts about the process of creating a PLC in the chart below.

Shared Purpose and Student Learning: Mission, Vision, Values, and Goals   What can I do?
Learning Teams: Collaborative Teamwork, Teacher Capacity, Leadership Capacity, Professional Development   How can I make this happen?
Reflection and Action: Continuous Learning and Improvement   What method(s) will I use?
Next Steps   What will I do next?

SUMMARY

The PLC principal leads a school that has embraced the shared purpose of improving student achievement. Together, administrators and their faculties develop an infrastructure of collaborative teamwork, producing an exciting synergy that effects change. Teacher capacity building and leadership capacity building are continuous, as the PLC nurtures the development and use of strategies and actions that increase the collective power, or efficacy, of the whole organization to engage in continuous improvement for ongoing student learning. Professional development, both external to the school and job-embedded within collaborative teams, supports the cycle of continuous learning that energizes a PLC. In an effective PLC, the principal and faculty take mutual responsibility for effectiveness, build a foundation of trust within the PLC together, accept mutual responsibility for interpersonal effectiveness, and consciously create a collaborative infrastructure. The resulting interpersonal synergy helps educators to plan creatively, respond to challenges proactively, and feel a collective sense of efficacy about the work they do.

What are the leadership practices that improve schools? Chapter 2, The Role of the Principal in Leading Professional Learning Communities, offers a framework of effective practices that principals demonstrate in their roles as PLC leaders.

The Role of the Principal in Leading Professional Learning Communities

The principal has an essential role in building a PLC in the school. Learning about the attributes of a PLC as described in Chapter 1 and making a decision to create a PLC in the school is only the first stage of the building process. The next stage of initiating the development of a PLC with staff requires careful planning and an understanding of the leadership practices that support principals in a successful implementation process.

This chapter is based on a leadership construct developed by Leithwood et al. (2006) in Chapter 2, The Nature of Successful Leadership Practices, of *Successful School Leadership*. These authors synthesized research from a number of sources and presented four core practices of successful leaders: setting directions, developing people, redesigning the organization, and managing the instructional program. Principals who consider these practices as they implement PLCs in their schools will provide the kind of support that nurtures the growth of professional learning communities.

Principals of PLCs are learners among learners. In their roles as instructional leaders, effective administrators model an understanding of both the theory and practical application of collaborative inquiry and action. This chapter provides principals with the opportunity to reflect on their own practice as leaders and apply this knowledge to the actual PLC implementation process in their schools.

LEADERSHIP PRACTICES OF THE PLC PRINCIPAL

Setting Directions: Shared Purpose

One of the principal's most important roles is setting directions for the school. Members of the staff are unlikely to come to the principal and ask to start a PLC in the school. Usually it is the principal through professional reading, professional development experiences, and networking with colleagues who becomes convinced of the value of establishing a PLC. Sometimes system leaders at the district level have made the building of PLCs a vehicle for meeting the priorities of the system. No matter the source of the initiative, it is the principal who makes the difference by setting the school's direction toward starting the collaborative culture of a PLC. Building shared mission, vision, value, and goal statements is not a new task for principals, but developing these statements to reflect the attributes of a PLC does require careful planning.

Principals have to introduce the concept of a PLC to school leaders and convince them of the value of the PLC model. This approach results in a PLC leadership team that supports the principal in setting the school direction. This leadership team could be named the PLC Steering Team. For the staff to be willing to accept the PLC initiative, they must learn about the attributes of PLCs. Staff are more receptive to learning about PLCs when the principal and teacher-leaders facilitate meetings to consider the value of creating a PLC in the school.

The principal fosters the acceptance of group goals by setting goals collaboratively and communicating them in a variety of ways. Communicating regularly with staff on the collaborative process of building a PLC is an essential practice of the PLC leader. Talking and writing continuously to staff about the values and goals of the PLC initiative is one way of doing this. The principal should constantly keep the school pointed toward its goal of becoming an effective PLC within the view of the staff. This will help the staff to see that the principal has high expectations of their commitment to developing the attributes of a PLC. Principals can create productive relations with families and communities by sharing PLC goals with students and parents in a newsletter. Everyone within the school community can contribute to building the PLC if they understand the value of the direction the school is taking.

The pathway to improved student achievement, improved teacher capacity, and improved leadership skills is constructed by the principal by setting the direction and then utilizing a variety of strategies to get to the goal of continuous improvement.

Developing People: Continuous Improvement

According to Leithwood et al. (2006), another core practice of successful leaders is developing people. The principal of a PLC understands the importance of supporting teachers in a collaborative culture. Leading change requires a principal who recognizes that every staff member is at a different stage in developing the attributes of the member of a PLC. Staff will need individualized support and consideration. When teachers trust their leaders, they are more open to taking a new pathway to building their instructional practice. The principal supports the learning required in initiating a PLC, not only with professional development but also by understanding the emotional needs of each staff member. The principal should continue to model the collaborative values and practices of a PLC leader.

To build a PLC is challenging. It takes thoughtful consideration of the value of a PLC in improving student achievement. It also requires an understanding of the key attributes of a PLC. Intellectual stimulation can be provided through professional learning opportunities focused on the attributes of a PLC. These may occur at staff meetings, in a book club, or within teacher learning teams once they are set up. Chapter 5 provides several strategies principals can use to develop the capacity of staff to function as an effective PLC. Principals can share resources such as books, journals, and articles or lead a book club on a book such as this one. In general, resources should be offered to support professional growth.

Another way to develop people's capacity as continuous learners is to serve as a role model. PLC principals continue to build their own capacity to lead the PLC project by attending professional development opportunities and participating as members of collaborative teams themselves. When principals value professional growth, teachers are more likely to participate in professional development.

Redesigning the Organization: Collaborative Culture

The third area where principal practices make a difference when building a PLC is in redesigning the organization of the school. To develop a collaborative culture, principals must change the typically solitary instructional practice of teachers. By introducing the research that shows that PLCs improve schools and redesigning the way the school does business, the principal makes the change to a collaborative culture possible. The key is creating effective teacher learning teams. Structuring the organization to facilitate collaborative work is a priority in leading a PLC. Providing time for teacher learning teams to meet to address student needs and improve instructional practice is the scaffold for improving schools. Resources must be provided to support the collaborative action of teacher learning teams. Four of the case studies in the Principal's Toolkit section at the back of this book provide examples of how principals successfully redesigned their schools to function as effective PLCs.

Managing the Instructional Program: The Principal as Instructional Leader

The most important role of the principal of a PLC is to manage the instructional program. Student achievement will not improve without instructional improvement. Therefore, the principal provides a school organized around teacher learning teams where improving instruction is their business. The principal provides resources to support collaborative instructional practice. The kind of professional learning opportunities that improve instructional practice are assessed and accessed by PLC leaders.

Every step the principal takes in building a PLC contributes to the practice of an effective instructional leader. From laying the foundations of mission, vision, values, and goals to setting up learning teams supported by the pillars of collaborative teamwork, teacher capacity, leadership capacity, and professional development, principals develop their skills as instructional leaders.

The knowledge and skills that matter in leadership, according to Elmore (2004), "are those that can be connected to, or lead directly to, the improvement of instruction and student performance" (p. 14). Since the purpose for creating the PLC infrastructure of collaborative action is to provide a process to improve instructional practice and raise student achievement, instructional leadership is at the heart of the successful implementation of a professional learning community.

Research has established that leadership is second only to classroom instruction when it comes to contributing to student achievement (Leithwood, Seashore Louis, Anderson, & Wahlstrom, 2004). If this is so, how can principals support the instructional program most effectively? Principals should be familiar with the best professional practices and support staff in their classroom use of the most effective instructional and professional practices that have an impact on student learning. There is a strong connection between capacity-building, instructional leadership and the development of PLCs. To provide instructional leadership, principals need professional development to enhance their knowledge and skills as to what effective instructional practice looks like in the classroom. They need to know how to analyze data and effectively manage evidence-based decision making. If principals want strong instructional practice from their teachers, principals need to model their commitment to professional growth for themselves. The PLC principal, model enthusiasm for his or her own professional learning about leadership practices, instructional strategies, and data analysis. Then in collaborative professional discussion with staff, the role of the principal as instructional leader is respected. In the PLC school, professional learning is a collaborative activity expected by all members of the school.

Leading the instructional program in a PLC means setting directions, building collaborative relationships, developing the instructional and leadership qualities of teachers, and managing the instructional program. Principals apply these practices within their roles as instructional leaders.

PRINCIPAL/VICE PRINCIPAL LEARNING TEAMS

One way in which school leaders can support each other as instructional leaders is to form their own principal learning teams with other principals in their school district. The advent of school leaders meeting across districts as learning teams is an exciting development in the area of capacity building across the system. To meet its standards for staff development, NSCD (2001) proposes that

administrator learning communities also meet on a regular basis to deepen participants' understanding of instructional leadership, identify practical ways to assist teachers in improving the quality of student work, critique one another's school improvement efforts, and learn important skills such as data analysis and providing helpful feedback to teachers. ("Learning Communities: The Rationale")

If principals in several schools in the district are determined to build PLCs, meeting as a principal learning team has powerful effects, because they can offer each other support in the implementation of professional learning communities in their schools. As a principal learning team, principals can access professional development as a group from the district and learn from each other in a situation that provides opportunities for collaborative action. Being part of a learning team with colleagues also helps principals to understand that collaborative teamwork is not easy. It takes hard work and commitment to the goals of the group. Principals have a better understanding of relationships of trust in teacher learning teams because trust is also needed in learning teams of administrators.

Case Study 5: Learning Teams for Principals and Vice Principals can be found in the Principal's Toolkit section at the back of the book. This case study describes a vice principal learning team and includes a copy of the proposal these school leaders made to their district for funding. The case study serves as an example of what school leaders can create for themselves to enhance their professional learning.

Reflection and Action Template

At this point in the chapter, principals are invited to reflect on the leadership practices they will rely on to implement PLCs by completing the PLC Leadership Practices Chart. (A full-page template can be found in the Principal's Toolkit: Reproducibles on page 109.) This chart is designed to help principals to reflect on the practices that research has found to be characteristic of successful leaders: setting directions, developing people, redesigning the organization, and managing the instructional program (Leithwood et al., 2006). The left-hand column lists the four leadership practices. In the column labeled "Reflection," principals are invited to state what practices they are already using in their schools. In the column labeled "Action," principals consider what practices they could initiate that would support their roles as leaders of PLCs. This process of reflection and then planning for action as a leader prepares the principal for the first stage of building a PLC—planning.

Core Practices of Successful Leaders*	Reflection *What practices are already in my leadership repertoire?*	Action *What practices will I act on as a PLC leader?*
Setting Directions		
Developing People		
Redesigning the Organization		
Managing the Instructional Program		

*SOURCE: Leithwood et al., 2006.

SUMMARY

When principals ensure that there is a continuous school focus on student achievement and make everyone accountable for student learning, the conditions for a collaborative culture are created. Expecting the instructional program to be developed by teacher learning teams and allocating resources to support collaborative action that benefits student learning is an effective strategy for encouraging an effective PLC.

The next four chapters of this book provide principals with a variety of practical strategies that support their work as instructional leaders in the start-up of a PLC. In the next chapter, a variety of strategies and tools for planning the PLC implementation process is provided.

CHAPTER 3

Planning for Professional Learning Communities

Getting started as a professional learning community leader requires planning. Once principals have an understanding of current research on professional learning communities, the seven attributes of a PLC, and the leadership practices of PLC leaders, they are ready to act to create the PLC culture of collaboration that will support student learning in their schools.

In this chapter, principals are introduced to several planning strategies that help to set up the conditions for laying the foundations of shared purpose and student learning, building the pillars that support learning teams, and raising the roof of continuous learning. These planning strategies are designed to be practical and quickly completed. Each reinforces the necessary conditions needed for successful implementation of PLCs. These strategies include setting up the PLC Steering Team, the PLC Snapshot Assessment, the PLC Portfolio, and the PLC Learning Grid. These strategies provide a collaborative leadership framework, an assessment rubric for the school PLC, a tracking tool to record accomplishments, and a chart to support continuous learning.

COLLABORATIVE LEADERSHIP: CREATING A PLC STEERING TEAM

A collaborative team of the principal and teacher representatives provides the best vehicle for creating the environment that is necessary for an effective learning community. When the principal shares decision making about PLCs with teacher-leaders, involving them in the planning and implementation of a PLC model in the school, a powerful force for change is unleashed (Fullan, 2006). Creating a professional learning community is best supported by a school leadership team that steers the implementation of the PLC infrastructure within the school—the PLC Steering Team.

This collaborative leadership team might evolve in several ways. Perhaps the principal is the first to consider the value of developing the school as a PLC, or it might be a teacher who approaches the principal with a proposal for implementing PLCs. Or it might be the district or system leaders who have proposed the PLC model on a districtwide basis. No matter the source of the original PLC proposal, the principal is responsible for setting the direction of the school and subsequent planning for a PLC.

If the idea is initiated by the principal, bringing together a team of teacher-leaders at the earliest stage of planning for a PLC promises the best chance of successful implementation. In this scenario, the principal will want to introduce these school leaders to PLCs. This handbook might be one way of doing this. A variety of articles and other books about PLCs can also be used. Districts sometimes bring in guest speakers or provide funding for teachers to attend workshops or conferences that focus on PLCs. The principal initiates the PLC Steering Team in this scenario. Allowing a leadership team time to reflect on the value of PLCs and then leading the team in getting started on the planning of the school PLC is an essential role of the principal.

If the staff initiates the conversation about PLCs, a major step toward implementation has already been made. The principal's role is then to support wholeheartedly the work of the school leaders in developing the PLC culture in the school.

Once the PLC Steering Team has been formed, the principal serves as the chair of this collaborative team. This team's mandate is to plan and begin the implementation process of developing a

PLC culture in the school. The PLC Steering Team has the important role of informing and motivating the staff to engage in the collaborative practices that improve instructional practice and student achievement. Establishing and overseeing the progress of effective learning teams is an essential role of the PLC Steering Team. When the principal shares the leadership role, collective power is fueled by the synergy of collaborative action.

PLC SNAPSHOT ASSESSMENT

The PLC Snapshot Assessment is a tool to help the principal and PLC Steering Team review the school against a set of criteria that describe a professional learning community. This snapshot serves as both a diagnostic assessment and an ongoing check of progress in meeting the goal of establishing a PLC in the school. The first PLC Snapshot Assessment is best taken as the PLC Steering Team begins the process of developing a PLC. Subsequent snapshot assessments could involve the whole staff, occurring at appropriate intervals over several years as the attributes of a PLC are developed over time.

The PLC Assessment Snapshot (see Figure 3.1) is a rubric with which the PLC Steering Team can measure where the school is in terms of meeting the criteria of a PLC. At the beginning of the planning process, this assessment tool answers the question, Where are we as a PLC? The table is divided into five columns:

1. Criteria

2. Stage 1: Knowledge (theory/concept attainment)

3. Stage 2: Application (action, ongoing efforts)

4. Stage 3: Accomplishments (results, products)

5. Reflection and Action: Review data; refocus, revise, renew plans

The first column lists the criteria of a PLC as presented in Figure 1.1, the PLC Edifice. Stage 1 is the knowledge stage, where school leaders and staff are getting to know the characteristics of PLCs. In Stage 2, collaborative teams have been set up, and team members have created action plans and begun the process of

Figure 3.1   PLC Snapshot Assessment

School: _____

Completed by: _____

Date: _____

Criteria	Stage 1 Knowledge	Stage 2 Application	Stage 3 Accomplishment	Reflection and Action
Shared Purpose of Student Learning				
Mission, Vision, Values, Goals				
Learning Teams				
Collaborative Teamwork				
Teacher Capacity				
Leadership Capacity				
Professional Development				
Continuous Learning and Improvement				
Reflection and Action				
Celebration				

improving student learning through data-based inquiry methods. Stage 3 provides the opportunity to access the results of the learning teams as applied to student, teacher, and leader learning. The final column allows the leadership team and staff to reflect on the level of implementation of each attribute of a PLC and plan subsequent actions.

At what point in the implementation process should the PLC Snapshot Assessment be introduced? Once the principal has formed the PLC Steering Team and supported them in under-standing the attributes of a PLC, the Snapshot Assessment is an important tool for their implementation plan. Since the PLC Snapshot Assessment is designed to fit the model introduced in Chapter 1 of this book, it is important that each member of the leadership team understand the attributes of a PLC represented in the PLC Edifice. Of course, this knowledge would be supplemented by readings and professional development from other sources.

This rubric can be adapted to suit an individual school's needs. The PLC Steering Team could adapt the table by using school specific attributes in the criteria column. The tool can be used as a checklist to indicate what stage the school is at as imple-mentation begins and continues. A more valuable use of the tool is to create it in an expandable Word document. Then the steering team can record evidence of where the school is in the appropriate squares. The final column, "Reflection and Action," is most important. In this column, the leadership team has the opportu-nity to create an action plan.

Besides serving as a diagnostic and planning tool, the PLC Snapshot Assessment also provides a record of the progress the school is making as it becomes a PLC. It has a place in the school's PLC Portfolio where the school's journey to becoming a PLC is recorded.

SETTING UP A TRACKING SYSTEM: THE PLC PORTFOLIO

The PLC Portfolio provides a record of all the school's accomplish-ments as it grows as a PLC. Assembling this portfolio is the respon-sibility of the PLC Steering Team. The PLC Portfolio presents the school as it is as it begins its journey into collaborative action for student learning and records the milestones as the PLC flourishes. At the beginning, it is a planning tool. As time goes by, it becomes a school self-assessment tool. Best of all, the PLC Portfolio is an instrument of celebration as the school reflects on the successes that mark its progress.

A PLC Portfolio provides the school with the opportunity to do the following:

- Assess the school in regards to the criteria of a PLC
- Provide a record of the school's growth as a PLC
- Showcase the accomplishments of the school as a PLC

To create a PLC Portfolio, do the following:

- Decide on a format (e.g., a binder divided into sections, electronic folders online).
- Decide on sections (e.g., Foundations, Learning Teams, Reflection and Action, and Celebration).

Recording and Planning for Continuous Learning: The PLC Learning Grid

The PLC Learning Grid, a short version of which appears below, is a note-taking tool that can assist the learner in recording significant ideas and strategies for the study and implementation of the attributes of a PLC. (A full-page template can be found in the Principal's Toolkit: Reproducibles on page 111.) Principals can quickly brainstorm and consider some practical applications of the knowledge and strategies encountered in their study of professional learning communities. In the first two columns, principals can jot down key ideas and the strategies that would be useful in their school contexts. The most important column is the last one, "Ways I Can Use ..." It provides the opportunity to move from theory to practice. The PLC Learning Grid lends itself to the process of recording initial learning and planning for change.

Following are further opportunities to use the note-taking and planning function of the PLC Learning Grid:

- As a tool while reading this book or other print and electronic resources
- During a staff meeting for professional development purposes
- During the planning process by a member of the PLC Steering team
- By a teacher in a learning team to provide the team with a tool to summarize and apply their learning

You may wish to photocopy the PLC Learning Grid to facilitate note taking as you read each chapter of the book. The chart is also easy to create as a table in an expandable Word document.

PLC Learning Grid		
Knowledge/Key Ideas	*Strategy/Activity*	*Ways I Can Use . . .*

SUMMARY

The successful implementation of a PLC requires careful planning. In this chapter, principals are advised to create a PLC Steering Team who will share leadership of the PLC initiative, reflecting the value of collaborative leadership. This team can assist in assessing the starting point for the school as it determines its needs as a PLC. The PLC Snapshot Assessment serves this function; it will also serve in the ongoing cycle of assessment of the school's progress in achieving its goals as a PLC.

The PLC Portfolio provides a vehicle for tracking the growth of the school as a PLC. It is set up at this stage on the understanding that it will become the showcase of accomplishments as the school develops the attributes of a PLC.

The PLC Learning Grid, a template for recording significant ideas and strategies from the chapter, is introduced at the end of the chapter. It is also designed to be used as a planning tool as readers respond to the prompt in the third column: "Ways I Can Use . . ." As well, the PLC Learning Grid appears at the end of each of the remaining chapters.

In Chapter 4, the building of a PLC begins. Principals are offered a variety of hands-on activities, including two Professional Development Modules, which will facilitate introduction of the attributes of a PLC with staff and the development of mission, vision, values, and goal statements for the emerging PLC.

CHAPTER 4

Introducing Staff to Professional Learning Communities

Foundations

Building any structure requires planning, but eventually the day comes for the ground breaking. In previous chapters, principals were introduced to the theoretical underpinnings of PLCs and learned about some preliminary planning tools for the principal and PLC Steering Team. In this chapter, principals are offered a variety of strategies that facilitate the collaborative construction of the foundations of a PLC with their staff. The hands-on activities of this chapter, along with the focus on establishing learning teams in later chapters, are designed to support principals as they introduce PLCs to staff and build enthusiasm for collaborative action.

Also introduced in this chapter, principals will find the two Professional Development (PD) Modules, "Laying the Foundations of Mission, Vision, Values, and Goals" and "Celebration," especially useful. In these modules (found at the back of the book in the Principal's Toolkit), workshop outlines provide step-by-step directions for introducing the foundations of a PLC and celebrating the process. Ready-made templates and scripts facilitate the delivery of the workshops at a staff meeting or PD session. These strategies work well for adult learners and have been used successfully in workshop situations to introduce the essential attributes of a professional learning community to a school.

LAYING THE FOUNDATIONS OF A PLC

The principal has a central role in laying the foundations of a PLC. Whether alone or with a leadership team, such as the PLC Steering Team, the principal is responsible for setting directions and developing people—two core practices of successful leaders (Leithwood et al., 2006). *Setting directions* involves working with the staff to create the mission, vision, values, and goals that support shared purpose and student learning in a PLC. *Developing people* requires the effective employment of the knowledge, skills, and attitudes that support people in making changes to the way they practice as professionals. The Professional Development Modules "Laying the Foundations of Mission, Vision, Values, and Goals" and "Celebration" in the Principal's Toolkit offer school leaders a variety of activities to choose from as they introduce staff to the foundational attributes of a PLC. Finally, the learning supports of a set of guiding questions on the foundations of a PLC and a PLC Learning Grid complete the chapter.

As the architect of the learning culture of the school, the principal builds a professional learning community upon the resilient foundations of mission, vision, values, and goals. Principals may have to reassess their prior knowledge about these concepts and be open to examine these foundations with a more focused lens and purpose, targeting student improvement and achievement. The commitment principals make to develop school improvement plans based upon these four elements will define the authenticity of the progress made and the success achieved.

Principals and staff choose to become PLCs when they are convinced of the value of this collaborative structure in making a difference to the learning of their students. When all educators in the school have the shared purpose of building the school's capacity to improve student learning and achievement, the motivation to become a PLC inspires the action necessary to make it happen. The principal's role in leading the staff through a reexamination of the mission, vision, values, and goals of the school is an important step in laying the foundation of a PLC. This process results in a blueprint that will guide the subsequent step of building a PLC—establishing learning teams.

Mission

The development of a mission statement is a common practice within organizations. As leaders of educational organizations, principals have not only read many of them but have authored many of their own. Regardless of geography, mission statements share common traits and belief statements. Simply stated, mission statements proclaim that schools believe that all students can learn and that their purpose is to help students be successful in the classroom and in the community. Mission statements demand purpose, clarity, and accountability.

Within a professional learning community, DuFour and Eaker (1998) believe that the development of a mission statement must include discussion and clarification of these fundamental questions: Why do we exist? What are we here to do together?

In a professional learning community, mission statements clarify what students will learn, how this learning will be assessed, and how educators will respond when students do not learn.

Vision

Vision statements provide a sense of direction. The articulation of the vision of a school is the setting down of the image of the future that the school wants to build. If a school modeled on the principles of a PLC is desired, then the vision statement says exactly what this looks like. This vision blueprint will support the school as it allocates time, resources, and shared personal commitment to constructing a vision of the future in concrete terms.

In a PLC, the vision statement focuses on intended results. It is developed collaboratively and has the strength of reflecting the shared purpose of all educators in the school. The school's vision statement serves as a key element of the foundations of school improvement.

A school's vision answers these questions: What will our school look like if improving student learning is our mission? How will we assess our success in achieving this vision? Together, the school's mission and vision reflect a shared purpose to improve student learning for all students.

Values

Identifying core values helps the school community to determine how it can make its vision of the future a reality. How must all educators in the school behave to achieve the school's mission? To build a PLC culture, principals and staff work together to build consensus and clearly define the values that underlie their commitment to the mission and vision statements they have created. If one of the school's value statements is "All students can learn," then the next step is to develop goals to support this value. Principals and all members of the educational community of the school are prompted into action on behalf of student learning when shared mission, vision, and values motivate them to create goals that inspire improvement.

The significance of shared values is an essential component of organizational effectiveness. Effective leaders clarify, share, and communicate the values of their schools (DuFour & Eaker, 1998). The significance of identifying and establishing shared values within schools is very clear. In a PLC, principals support all individuals who have a direct impact on student learning and success by demonstrating their commitment to the values underpinning the mission and vision that have been collaboratively developed.

Goals

Laying the foundation of a PLC is especially dependent on setting goals that are linked to the mission, vision, and values developed by the school. Collaborative action to improve student learning cannot occur without goals, action plans, and a strategy to assess how well the goals are being met. Goal setting is similar to creating blueprints for the PLC. Goals describe actions that can be monitored and measured. Prioritizing goals identifies what needs to be accomplished first and then what needs to be done next. Time lines for the implementation of strategies to achieve these goals must be realistic and include review dates to assess progress. Some school goals will be broad with long-term outcomes; however, in a PLC, the most effective goals are designed specifically to create short-term gains. Incremental steps of success energize the commitment, the persistence, and the patience required to achieve long-term goals (Conzemius & O'Neill, 2002).

The school improvement process is a journey. Maps, guideposts, and compasses are needed along the way. The monitoring and measuring of progress is a crucial step throughout the improvement process. Having only a limited number of goals allows the school to measure small and consistent gains. When goals are very specific, they can be measured and effectively managed.

Conzemius and O'Neill (2002) propose that developing SMART goals is one effective method of improving student achievement. The acronym describes a goal-setting process where the goals are **S**pecific, **M**easurable, **A**ttainable, **R**esults oriented, and **T**ime bound. DuFour and Eaker (1998) suggest that goals be linked to the school vision and monitored continuously to make sure that they are accomplishing the desired outcomes that all members of the school community have endorsed. Some goals are designed for the school as a whole to achieve; others, especially those designed by PLC teacher learning teams, are specific to their own students.

In a PLC, goal setting is a very detailed and comprehensive activity, requiring the school continually to reflect and assess how the goal statements support and promote the mission, vision, and values of the school.

**Professional Development Modules:
Introducing Staff to PLCs**

As with any new initiative being introduced to a school, a variety of approaches can be taken. Sometimes outside experts are invited to share their expertise. In this handbook, however, the principal's role as instructional leader is actively supported. Principals are invited to tailor the strategies and activities found in the PD Module to suit the context of their schools.

As soon as the topic of PLCs is raised, different staff members will be knowledgeable about them to various degrees. Some will know little about them, some will have read about or heard about them, and some may have been a member of a PLC in another setting. Naturally, staff will want their principals to answer the same questions principals posed as they picked up this handbook: What is a PLC? Why should the school become a PLC? Who is responsible for developing the school as a PLC? How does the school create the collaborative culture of a PLC? How does the school sustain itself as a PLC over time? The manner in which PLCs are introduced to the staff is an important element of eventual adoption and sustainability.

As instructional leaders, principals sometimes provide staff development sessions for the teachers or work collaboratively with a teacher leadership team in designing and delivering staff development sessions. The PLC Steering Team may fill this role. These professional development sessions may be one-day workshops, half-day training sessions, or a one-hour portion of each staff meeting that is devoted to staff development. This handbook emerged from the outline of a one-day workshop on PLCs in which hundreds of Ontario principals and vice principals have participated.

In making use of the "Laying the Foundations of Mission, Vision, Values, and Goals" PD and "Celebration" PD Modules, principals are invited to mix and match introductory strategies for getting started on building PLCs. In Chapter 5, a third PD Module is introduced (The PD modules can be found in the Principal's Toolkit: Professsional Development Modules, starting on page 67.) for establishing learning teams. All of the PD Modules in this book are designed to be facilitated by the principal and/or the school PLC Steering Team.

GUIDING QUESTIONS

The questions that follow are another tool for school leaders who are planning to create a professional learning community in their schools. Principals could choose the questions that would serve their needs in planning. Perhaps a principal could use several of these questions to start the process at a staff meeting. Or a set of questions could be the starting point for discussions of articles and books about professional learning communities. Some of these questions will help with the organizational and practical aspects of setting up an environment that supports a professional learning community in the school. Principals could read the list and highlight the questions that might serve them best as they create a professional learning community. From there, principals could make their own planning templates or work together with a PLC team to develop their own planning tools that suit the nature of particular schools.

These questions are designed to help principals in the planning process as they work on laying the foundations that support the shared purpose of improving student learning: mission, vision, values, and goals. Principals might ask these questions before, during, and after introducing the PLC foundations teams to the staff.

1. Describe an ideal school where the central focus is student learning. What does it look like? What are people doing? What is the leader doing?

2. Does the school's mission statement focus on student learning, and is it stated in a clear, measurable way so that student success/failure can be readily measured?

3. Brainstorm any challenges that exist in the school. Cluster them into common areas and give them an overall focus title. How can the school's mission, vision, and value statements help to meet those challenges?

4. What are the indicators that a school is a professional learning community?

5. What are the behaviors of school leaders in a learning community?

6. What is the principal doing? What are the teachers doing?

7. If what matters is improving student learning, then what really is most important? How does a school leader help a staff to discover what is most important? How does a leader help a staff to recognize their purpose, their shared values, and their student learning goals?

8. List what matters to you and describe steps you will take to gain consensus on mission, vision, values, and goals.

9. How can the school work collaboratively to lay the foundations of a PLC?

Recording and Planning for Continuous Learning: The PLC Learning Grid

A PLC Learning Grid for Chapter 4 appears below. (A full-page template can be found in the Principal's Toolkit: Reproducibles on page 111.) It is a tool to record learning and the ways school leaders and teachers can use the activities and strategies outlined in this chapter to build the foundations of a PLC in the school. You may wish to photocopy the PLC Learning Grid before you begin your reading. Principals can also use the PLC Learning Grid with staff when facilitating the PD Module in this chapter. A more detailed explanation of the use of the PLC Learning Grid is found in Chapter 3.

PLC Learning Grid		
Knowledge / Key Ideas	*Strategy / Activity*	*Ways I Can Use . . .*

SUMMARY

Building a professional learning community requires schools to examine and respond to the key questions surrounding the four foundations of mission, vision, values, and goals. As instructional leaders, principals must begin this journey with an understanding and commitment to a very challenging process. The many challenges principals face each day are equaled only by the many opportunities they have to engage others and themselves in the learning process. Patience and persistence will keep principals on course. A positive attitude, a sense of humor, and a celebration of the smaller gains along the journey will help school leaders to model and to sustain the enthusiasm and the commitment they have made to the shared purpose of improving student learning in their school.

In this chapter, principals are provided with a variety of practical strategies, activities, and tools that can be adapted to suit the context of their schools. Laying the foundations of mission, vision, values, and goals as a collaborative effort and seeing evident action facilitates the next stage of raising the pillars that support learning teams.

In Chapter 5, principals are offered practical tools to work with their staff to raise the pillars that support learning teams: collaborative teamwork, teacher capacity, leadership capacity, and professional development.

CHAPTER 5

Supporting
Learning Teams

The Pillars

Once the foundations of the PLC are in place, it's time to build the pillars that support effective teacher learning teams: collaborative teamwork, teacher capacity, leadership capacity, and professional development. A PLC organizes its instructional program around an infrastructure of teacher learning teams. This chapter begins with answers to the what, why, and how questions of learning teams. A discussion of the four pillars that support collaborative action for student achievement follows. The third Professional Development Module is introduced in this chapter, "PLC Learning Teams." This PD Module is designed to introduce staff to the concept of an instructional program based on learning teams. It contains several interactive activities and suggested scripts that principals can use as is or adapt.

The jigsaw activity in the PD Module is supported by four case studies, which are also found in the Principal's Toolkit at the back of the handbook: "Leading and Learning in Teams in an Elementary School," "Implementing a Professional Learning Community in a Secondary School," "Learning Teams in an Elementary School," and "One School's Journey: SMART Goals for Student Success in a Middle School." These case studies are written by school administrators who share their experiences in setting up learning teams and school cultures that support professional learning communities. Principals might want to adapt the original templates of staff memos for their own use.

This chapter presents an extremely important stage in building the PLC Edifice. Without constructing the strong pillars of collaborative action, teacher capacity, leadership capacity, and professional development, learning teams are unsupported, and the professional learning community cannot be initiated and sustained.

LEARNING TEAMS FOR IMPROVING STUDENT ACHIEVEMENT

What Are Learning Teams?

To support the building of a professional learning community, the principal must create a collaborative culture that places learning first—the learning of administrators, teachers, and students. Research has shown that learning teams can be an extremely effective method of improving instruction and student achievement (Schmoker, 2005). A learning team provides a forum for building knowledge, planning, testing ideas, and reflecting together.

A learning team is not simply a group of individuals who get together periodically to talk about what is happening. Nor is it a book club that gathers to discuss what an author said or a committee to solve operational issues in the school. Rather, a learning team is a small group of professionals who agree to experiment with new ideas and meet regularly for a specific period of time to share specific professional growth experiences guided by specific goals and purposes. Learning team meetings are times for sharing lessons learned in the classroom and reflecting on the application of new knowledge and skills as they impact student learning. Learning team meetings are structured to share successes and discuss strategies that worked in the classroom, as well as to share difficulties, determine why they arose, and find solutions.

Why Are Learning Teams Essential to a PLC?

Successfully functioning learning teams provide excellent professional development, building a deeper understanding of how students learn and the teaching strategies that improve student achievement.

Learning teams do the following:

- Provide for the study of new ideas and current research.
- Offer the opportunity for teachers to experiment with new ideas in the classroom and monitor their success by examining student achievement data.
- Encourage the pooling of ideas and experience to solve challenges collaboratively.

Learning teams provide the opportunity for effective professional growth because they rely on the powerful principles of collaborative learning. Learning teams also model the kind of learning environment that should exist in every classroom and school environment, wherein learners do the following:

- Begin learning with a sense of what they already know.
- Learn at their own individual rates.
- Take the risk of trying new ideas.
- Monitor their success.
- Maintain records of their improving competence and confidence.
- Feel a sense of personal accomplishment as they grow.

Learning teams provide the structural support for the development of a professional learning community. The four pillars of collaborative teamwork, teacher capacity, leadership capacity, and professional development are essential to creating a building that thrives on professional learning.

How Are Learning Teams Set Up?

There are several ways to set up learning teams in a school. When introducing the concepts of a professional learning community and the role of collaborative teams, take advantage of the variety of sources available. Following are some examples:

- Adapt the model provided in this handbook to suit the context of the school.

- Use the knowledge and skills developed by the PLC Steering Team in staff meetings, workshops, and in-school release time meetings to introduce and provide guidance for school learning teams.
- Read and consider the case studies and experiences of school leaders who have implemented effective learning teams in their schools.

Creating Time for Teachers to Collaborate in Learning Teams

Time for collaboration and teamwork is essential to establishing a school culture that supports a professional learning community. Teams need time to meet during the school day. Principals have used some of the following strategies to release teachers to work in their learning teams:

- *Timetable:* Grade teams have a scheduled planning time together for PLC collaboration.
- *Reading buddies:* Students in a higher grade read with younger students, freeing up the teacher(s) of the older students to meet in their learning teams. This is reciprocated the next week.
- *Guest speakers:* Students go to an assembly where they are supervised by the principal and support staff while their teachers meet in their learning teams.
- *Monthly focus on a social skill:* Have an assembly or show a film to free up staff, supervised as above.
- *Common teacher preparation time:* Build in one period per timetable cycle and combine it with one of the above suggestions.
- *Electives:* Offer curriculum-based electives for students and free up staff for a quarter day. Try to involve retired teachers to assist as volunteers to teach an elective.
- *Parallel scheduling:* Offer the same subject at the same time to show a film from a book studied in class to both classes and free up staff.
- *District-funded release time:* Apply for money to free teachers up for a half-day planning session.

THE FOUR PILLARS

Pillar One: Collaborative Teamwork

The pillar of collaborative teamwork is essential to building and supporting a professional learning community. Creating a collaborative culture is an important factor for accomplishing successful school improvement initiatives. Principals who plan to enhance student and staff effectiveness in their schools need to develop their expertise in implementing collaborative learning teams.

Since educators are concerned with learning for all, it is important to establish and sustain a school culture where collaboration is valued on all levels. Collaboration engages school leaders and teachers in team-building activities that develop respect and trust. By engaging in professional dialogue to acknowledge, identify, and actively address learning issues, the principal and teachers create a synergy that leads to improved educational practice.

An effective vehicle for collaboration is the organization of school staff into learning teams. Collaborative skills, such as participation, listening, communication, and conflict resolution, develop to a higher level in committed learning teams. Collaboration takes a commitment to the shared purpose of improving student achievement. Collaborative action requires skill in creating and implementing a plan, followed by assessment of the plan's success in meeting its learning goals. Effective collaboration requires a lot of planning, but it is worth the effort. As learning teams start up, members should consider the following:

- Team organization
- Decision making
- Managing meetings
- Sharing the workload
- Commitment of team members
- Establishing a record-keeping method
- Monitoring team progress

Once the learning teams are established, the participants then address the chosen task.

Educators who write about professional learning communities offer a variety of ways of going about this. The References section of this book offers some print resources for principals. The common thread that runs through these books is the need to establish goals, prioritize and assign tasks, monitor team progress, and respond actively to team results. The pillar of collaborative teamwork is essential to building and supporting a PLC.

Pillar Two: Teacher Capacity

While the ultimate goal of a professional learning community is improved student learning, this cannot happen without improved instructional practice. Building teacher capacity is therefore an essential pillar in the improvement process. The value of learning teams rests in the opportunity they provide for collective inquiry into instruction. Below is a list of practices used by effective learning teams that have a positive impact on teacher capacity:

- *Professional dialogue:* Members of the learning team talk and challenge each other about their assumptions and beliefs about student learning and their own learning in their classrooms.
- *Shared meaning:* The learning team arrives at common ground and shares insights into learning in their classrooms.
- *Joint planning:* The learning team designs action steps, an initiative to test their shared insights.
- *Coordinated action:* The learning team carries out the action plan. This action need not be joint action but can be carried out independently by the members of the team.
- *Reflection and review:* The learning team examines student achievement data as a result of the action plan and responds to results.

Collective inquiry takes the form of questioning the status quo—delving deeper into instructional practice and assessment design and looking for measurable evidence that learning has occurred. A professional learning community may involve subject teachers collaborating on selecting essential outcomes for their course, creating a common assessment, and then using this assessment to examine the successes and failures not only of their students but also of their instructional practices. Or it can take the form of having a group of division teachers examine literacy/ numeracy scores and create an action plan with SMART goals to ensure future success based on these results. Through this process of collective inquiry, school improvement can be identified, measured, and sustained. When a teacher team is encouraged to share its expertise and best practice beyond the team, the connections between teachers in different subject areas, divisions, schools, or districts are strengthened.

One important contribution of a PLC is that it creates the conditions that encourage teachers to open up their doors and their practice to the scrutiny of their colleagues. When members of a learning team research the effect of an instructional practice that the team feels will improve student learning, observing the lessons of colleagues becomes an opportunity to question, learn, and improve. The synergy of collaboration creates the trust necessary for teachers to take the risk of opening their practice to observation. One strategy that learning teams have used successfully to open classroom doors is "lesson study" (NSCD, 2004). Lesson study is a team activity where teachers collaboratively plan a lesson, which is then taught by one of the team members while the rest of the team observes the student learning responses. The team follows up with a joint review of the results of the instruction on student learning. Learning teams are a powerful vehicle to build teacher capacity. In the process of creating professional knowledge, school leaders and teachers in a PLC are likely to have a

readiness to tinker and experiment in an ad hoc way with new ideas, or variations on old ideas, in order to do things better, within a culture that does not blame individuals when things prove not to be good enough, mistakes being treated as opportunities for learning. (Hargreaves, 2001, p. 227)

When principals and teachers participate in the collective inquiry process, they become a community of learners. Also, an understanding and appreciation of each other's work is fostered. This collaborative approach to solving issues of student learning is not an easy process; however, it creates ties that bind the structure of learning together.

Pillar Three: Leadership Capacity

The third pillar that supports collaborative action is leadership capacity. Professional learning communities need effective leaders, both administrators and teacher-leaders. Shared leadership fosters a collaborative culture that bases school decisions on what is best for school improvement. Principals in PLCs demonstrate how much they value teacher team leaders and instructional experts, supporting them as they grow in leadership capacity. Professional learning communities nurture leadership capacity building at all levels.

Educational research presents the findings that school leadership is second only to classroom teaching as an influence on student achievement. In fact, without talented school leadership, schools cannot be turned around, and gains in student achievement do not happen (Leithwood et al., 2006). Principals of PLCs understand that improving teacher instructional practice is central to successful school leadership. PLC principals access a variety of professional learning opportunities and resources that build their leadership capacity.

Principals set directions when they introduce their staffs to the attributes of PLCs and show they value collaborative action to raise student achievement. When principals initiate a structure of teacher learning teams to lead the school instructional program, they are providing a rich environment for professional growth and teacher capacity building. Redesigning the organization to build a collaborative culture is best accomplished through principals actively supporting learning teams. Finally, principals in a PLC expertly manage the instructional program. Successful use of these practices builds the instructional leadership capacity of principals so that they can more effectively support teaching practices that impact on student achievement.

Principals who engage in professional learning opportunities to build their capacity as PLC leaders serve as inspirational models to their teachers. Instructional leadership requires active participation in a variety of professional development activities. Instructional expertise is needed by principals to supervise instructional programs that impact on student achievement. Beyond instructional expertise, principals in PLCs lead their teachers by providing expert support of teacher collaborative instructional practice. There is a strong connection between leadership capacity building, instructional leadership, and the development of effective learning communities.

Pillar Four: Professional Development

Another important support pillar of a professional learning community is professional development. It takes hard work, commitment, and skill to act successfully to improve leadership practice, teaching practice, and student achievement. A school organized for teacher learning promotes the systematic study of teaching and learning. Job-embedded professional development takes place as learning teams deliberate, act on their plans, and then assess the effectiveness of their experiments with instructional practices. Change in teaching practice cannot occur unless teachers are willing to put what they are discussing in their learning teams into action in the classroom. The work of collecting and evaluating student achievement data and then responding as a team is central to the effectiveness of a professional learning community.

The principal can facilitate action orientation in the following ways:

- Providing resources as teachers investigate questions, problems, and student learning issues that learning teams have recognized in their goals
- Developing the school learning culture to support the habit of sharing student assessment results and responding actively to improve future results
- Sharing responsibility for student learning and working collaboratively with the learning teams to achieve their goals
- Facilitating professional growth opportunities that support the development of knowledge and skills about action orientation in a professional learning community

Job-embedded professional development occurs as learning teams participate in collective inquiry practices where experimentation is valued. The goals of a learning team need to be translated into action and tested in the classroom. When members of learning teams research the impact of their own instructional practice, their learning is directly translated into classroom instruction. One model of a successful experimentation process is action research. *Action research* is an investigation carried out by teachers and principals in school settings to answer a question or gauge the impact of a strategy on improving student learning. Teachers study professional practices that research concludes will improve student learning and then experiment in their classrooms.

The teacher and learning team analyze the resulting data on student achievement and respond to the results.

The process of action research has proven to have a positive influence on what goes on in the classrooms. Teacher inquiry that is research based and data driven creates more effective classroom practice. Principals who conduct action research on their own leadership practice are committed to a process of professional learning that supports improved leadership and serves as a model to their teachers (Sagor, 2004). Experimentation provides a professional learning communication within its structure of inquiry.

Besides job-embedded professional development, principals and teachers in PLCs continue to access external sources of professional development. In a PLC, accessing knowledge and skills from outside sources results from a review of team goals. The expertise of educators outside the school includes access to the following resources:

- Colleagues in other schools, districts, or states/provinces
- Articles in educational journals and at online sites
- Books
- Multimedia materials
- Experts who provide face-to-face or online workshops
- Conferences, forums, and symposia

Ongoing professional development is an important pillar of learning teams that get results in improved instruction and a corresponding increase in student achievement. The role of the principal is to help teachers to access professional development that meets their needs as members of a PLC. At the same time, principals continue their own professional development.

Professional Development Module: PLC Learning Teams

The final PD Module found at the back of the book, Professional Development Module 3: PLC Learning Teams, is designed as an introduction to the role of learning naturally from the module on planning for PLCs. Several of the activities in PD Module 1 could be substituted for the introductory activities suggested in this PD Module. The PD modules can be found in the Principal's Toolkit: Professional Development Modules starting on page 67.

GUIDING QUESTIONS

The following questions are designed to help principals in the planning process as they work on the core leadership practice of redesigning the organization to establish PLC learning teams in their schools. Principals might ask these questions before, during, and after introducing PLC learning teams to the staff.

1. What structures are in place to help create or enhance the school's collaborative culture?

2. What team structures need to be created (e.g., grade, course, division, department, schoolwide) to analyze student learning and identify areas of need?

3. What steps will I (we) need to take to engage the staff in the concept of becoming a professional learning community? Which staff will be inspired by the possibilities?

4. How will I (we) follow the progress of the teams?

5. How will the teams implement the goals?

6. How will the teams monitor their own progress?

7. How will professional development be an integral part of the learning teams?

8. How many people will be on each team? What will be the mandate be for the teams? What evidence will be required for each team as a baseline for the learning? What support resources will I (we) supply?

9. How will sharing take place among the teams?

10. How will I (we) find collaborative time both within and without the school day?

11. How do I (we) support teacher and leadership capacity building?

Recording and Planning for Continuous Learning: The PLC Learning Grid

The PLC Learning Grid for Chapter 5 appears below. It is a tool to record your learning and the ways you can use the activities and strategies outlined in this chapter to create a professional learning community in your school. You may wish to photocopy the PLC Learning Grid before you begin your reading. Principals can also use the PLC Learning Grid with staff when facilitating the PD Module in this chapter. A more detailed explanation of the use of the PLC Learning Grid is found in Chapter 3.

PLC Learning Grid		
Knowledge / Key Ideas	*Strategy / Activity*	*Ways I Can Use . . .*

SUMMARY

This chapter provides principals with a variety of strategies and activities to support the establishment of PLC learning teams in their schools. The role, rationale, and set-up procedure for learning teams are outlined. As well, this chapter describes the vital supporting role of the four pillars of collaborative teamwork, teacher capacity, leadership capacity, and professional development. This theoretical information is matched with practical, hands-on material. A facilitator's guide to a Professional Development Module is provided that principals can use with staff to introduce and initiate PLC learning teams. Guiding questions are provided so principals can reflect before, during, and after the introduction of an instructional program based on collaborative action. The PLC Grid at the end serves as a tool to record learning.

A look at the PLC Edifice demonstrates how far along the building process has progressed once the school learning teams are up and running in the way they are intended to do. The next stage of the building process is described in Chapter 6. When the learning teams collaborate for action, maintain a results orientation, reflect, and respond to their findings, the cycle of continuous improvement characteristic of a PLC emerges. All along the way, the flag of celebration waves, as the shared purpose of improving student achievement is relentlessly pursued and accomplished.

Continuous Learning and Continuous Improvement

The Roof

The final stage of building a professional learning community is capping the pillars with the roof. Looking back over this book, we began by providing principals with tools to develop PLC plans, we set the foundations of a PLC by supporting principals as they introduce the concept of PLCs to their staffs, and then we constructed the pillars that support learning teams. In this chapter, the roof of sustainability is set upon the collaborative culture that has been built.

A PLC is characterized by a commitment to continuous learning and improvement that extends into the months and years that follow the implementation of the PLC culture. A cycle of continuous learning is set in place within the work of the learning teams and the school improvement process. The PLC school is results oriented and uses reflection on student achievement, teacher practice, and leadership practice as a catalyst to action. Finally, the flag of celebration caps the PLC edifice. For continuous learning and improvement to occur, the PLC principal supports the cycle of reflection and action, enhancing the school's collaborative efforts with ongoing celebration of achievement of every kind.

REFLECTION AND ACTION

Successful, continuous improvement of student achievement depends upon a long-term commitment to the collaborative environment created by principals and effective learning teams who conduct collective inquiry with positive results. Principals, teachers, and students benefit from this ongoing collaboration. When principals work together with their teacher learning teams, they share the challenges and successes of working continuously on improving student achievement. When teachers work together in collaborative teams, valuing themselves as continuous learners, they can build the same qualities into their classroom practice.

Creating a school improvement plan based on the PLC model is just one step on the road to continuous improvement. Results must be reviewed reflectively, plans revised, and efforts refocused and renewed. Principals foster continuous improvement by initiating and supporting a process of reflection and action. The five Rs of reflection and action—reflect, review, refocus, revise, and renew—produce the synergy that supports action for improvement at all levels of the school. For continuous learning to occur, on a cyclical basis, PLCs must do the following (see Figure 6.1):

- Reflect on and assess achievement of PLC goals.
- Review and respond to data from student achievement results.
- Refocus on mission, vision, values, and goals.
- Revise the school improvement plan, learning team plans, and teacher plans.
- Renew the collaborative efforts of leadership and learning teams.

Continue this reflection and action cycle into the future.

Figure 6.1   Reflection in Action Cycle

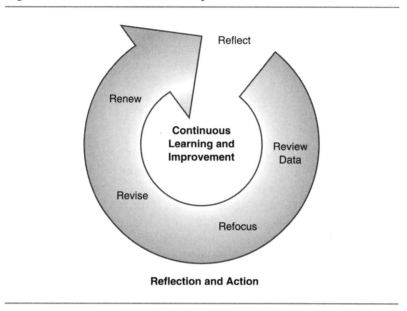

Reflect

Renew

Continuous Learning and Improvement

Review Data

Revise

Refocus

Reflection and Action

Reflect

Continuous learning and improvement is based on a cycle that starts with reflection. Successful PLC schools regularly assess their level of success in attaining their PLC goals. The principal provides opportunities for the whole school to reflect on how well the school is implementing the attributes of a PLC. The PLC Snapshot Assessment introduced in Chapter 3 is a useful tool to return to at set dates. The staff should decide the number of times a year they need to complete this snapshot of the school's progress toward becoming a PLC. The process of completing the PLC Snapshot Assessment is a powerful catalyst for reflection leading to action. The school improvement plan benefits from this reflective process as well.

At the instructional level, teacher learning teams provide teachers with forums for reflective dialogue. In PLCs, teacher teams support each other by jointly developing curriculum goals and assessment strategies, implementing new teaching strategies, consulting over problems, analyzing achievement data together, and responding with improved instruction. Reflection is built in, and the synergy of the joint effort is more likely to sustain an action-oriented response to student instructional needs. A reflective school culture has developed when teachers constantly ask the question: What do we do if this student doesn't learn?

Review Data

An essential ingredient of the reflection process is data. The PLC principal supports the staff in developing their knowledge and skill in reviewing, analyzing, and responding to data. Principals often access professional development opportunities to increase their own and their teachers' knowledge and skills in this area. The collection and use of data by principals and their staffs to determine school needs and to facilitate school improvement plans characterize a PLC.

Data can be collected from a number of sources. The completed PLC Snapshot Assessment provides data to review on the status of the school as a developing PLC.

At the instructional level of the teacher learning teams, review of student achievement data from a variety of sources is necessary. Diagnostic instruments, standardized tests, report cards, and examples of student work are among the forms of data available for analysis and response. Data-driven instructional practice is based on the premise that educators should develop the professional expertise to determine the instructional needs of every student. Many schools and districts are using goal-setting, review, and respond models such as the one mentioned earlier in this book, SMART goals, as a framework for planning.

The purpose of a cyclical review of data is twofold in a PLC. The data showcases the successes achieved by the whole school in achieving the goals of the school improvement plan and by each teacher learning team in improving student achievement. These successes provide opportunities for celebration. Secondly, data review clarifies areas where the school must improve as a PLC and where gaps in student achievement must be addressed. When instructional goals are not being met for some students, reviewing the data with the purpose of developing new instructional strategies for those students is an essential process in improving student learning.

Refocus

Along with leading the review of data, PLC principals are encouraged to keep the focus of the school on the school improvement plan and its commitment to building a PLC culture. Principals are responsible for setting directions and refocusing the staff when distractions lead them away from their PLC goals. Sustaining collaborative action requires principals constantly to communicate the school's mission, vision, values, and goals.

There must also be talk about the core values of the school, especially the commitment to raising student achievement—a good time to do this is during the review process. The expectation in PLCs is that all educators in the school must accept the ongoing collective responsibility to work together for student learning. Therefore, if the data indicate that new actions are needed in response to the findings, the principal leads the staff in reviewing the school improvement plan. This might take the form of returning to the fishbone graphic organizer shared in Professional Development Module 1 at the back of the book to refocus on the foundations of the PLC and make revisions to the plan.

Revise

The next step in the reflection and action cycle is to revise plans wherever necessary. This could involve revising the school improvement plan and learning team plans and individual teacher plans. The first set of goals developed collaboratively by the principal, PLC Steering Team, and staff to launch the construction of the PLC is reviewed, and adjustments are made in response. The action plan is revised as well. The same process is applied to the goals and instructional plans developed by the teacher learning teams. Finally, teachers make revisions to their own lessons in response to the data on student achievement. The willingness to adapt and change strategies in response to data is one of the reasons for the dynamic power of PLCs. They are built for collaborative action. The resulting synergy supports continuous learning and improvement.

Renew

Another important step is to renew the collaborative efforts of leadership and learning teams. The continuous cycle of reflection and action provides many opportunities to enjoy the challenge of striving for goals and celebrating their attainment. Where the plans did not work as well as expected, the review-and-revise process allows school leaders and teachers to adjust their plans. The principal leads this renewal process, offering gratitude and encouragement for the goals accomplished and resources for the continuing actions to raise student achievement.

CELEBRATION

There is much to celebrate in a professional learning community. The list below highlights some of the characteristics we see in a PLC school that is working well:

- Teachers and school leaders working in teams in a culture of inquiry and action
- Professional development opportunities for staff members that are translated into effective classroom practice
- Improvement in student achievement that is evidence informed by assessment literate teachers
- Principals and teachers who are learning together in a culture of respect, trust, and collective commitment to learning

These qualities of a PLC need to be nurtured on an ongoing basis.

Celebrating the accomplishments of teachers and students is an important role of the principal in a professional learning community. Celebrations foster a positive school culture—a significant factor in teacher work satisfaction and in student motivation. There are a number of reasons for using celebration, rituals, and stories to help foster the culture of a learning community. The flag of recognition and appreciation accomplishes the following:

- Makes the recipients feel good about their contribution to learning.

- Reinforces what the school values and signals what is important.
- Provides models of the values of the school at work and encourages others to act in accordance with those values.
- Keeps people contributing to collective endeavors.
- Encourages playfulness and fun.

Following are some tips for incorporating celebration into the culture of a school (DuFour & Eaker, 1998):

- Explicitly state why the celebration is needed.
- Make celebration everyone's responsibility.
- Establish a clear link between public recognition and the advancement of vision and values.
- Create opportunities for a lot of winners.

To recognize staff and student achievements, a principal can do the following:

- Involve the school council, the student council, and staff in designing a recognition program.
- Create a "recognition event."
- Schedule celebrations.
- Start small and celebrate each success.
- Have private as well as public rewards and recognition.
- Write thank-you notes.
- Keep a file of recognition ideas.
- Provide performance feedback on an ongoing basis.
- Recognize the variety of ways staff and students can be successful.
- Design new traditions and ceremonies that reflect the values of a professional learning community.
- Encourage the publication of articles that celebrate the accomplishments the staff and students of the school.

PLC Portfolio

Continuous learning and improvement are supported by recognition of the efforts of the whole school in building the attributes of a PLC. The PLC Portfolio, presented as a strategy in Chapter 3, is a very useful tool for showcasing the accomplishments of the staff. The PLC Steering Team has the responsibility of keeping a record of the actions of the school members as they move forward as a PLC. The whole school decides what should be included in the portfolio.

Items may include the following:

- PLC Snapshot Assessments, learning plans, and records of the reflection and action cycle
- Newsletters to the parent community about the accomplishments of the school as a PLC
- Accounts of special school events organized as part of meeting the goals of the school improvement plan
- Artifacts that demonstrate the achievement of students and outlines of instructional strategies that make a difference to student learning

The compilation and sharing of the PLC Portfolio with the school community reinforces the school's shared purpose of improving student achievement. Celebrate PLC learning in all its manifestations.

GUIDING QUESTIONS

Reflection and Action

Here are some questions that principals and teachers can ask themselves as part of the reflection and action process:

- How will I (we) promote systematic study of teaching and learning in the school?
- What data are available at the school for teachers to use in the reflection and action process (e.g., standardized test scores)?
- What forms of student assessment does the staff engage in that can be used in the reflection and action process (e.g., ongoing assessment in the classroom)?
- What will I (we) have to put in place at my (our) school for the staff to work together collaboratively?

- What do I (we) do in my (our) building to foster trust among the staff?
- How do I (we) ensure that teachers are reflecting on their work?
- How will teachers report the findings of their inquiries?
- How can I (we) provide time for the teachers to engage collaboratively in teacher inquiry?
- What common goals and beliefs does the staff need to engage in effective experimentation that will lead to improved student learning?
- What is my (our) time line for building a professional learning community?
- How will I (we) measure progress?

Celebration

- Do the symbols and signs at my (our) school reflect the celebratory nature of a professional learning community?
- What can I (we) do to celebrate as a professional learning community?
- How can the PLC Portfolio be used to celebrate the accomplishments of the school as a PLC?

Recording and Planning for Continuous Learning: The PLC Learning Grid

The PLC Learning Grid appears below (A full-page template can be found in the Principal's Toolkit: Reproducibles on page 111.). It is a tool to record your learning and the ways you can use the activities and strategies outlined in this chapter to reflect on and plan further actions in your PLC.

PLC Learning Grid		
Knowledge / Key Ideas	*Strategy / Activity*	*Ways I Can Use . . .*

SUMMARY

This handbook focuses mainly on supporting principals and school leadership teams as they get started on building a PLC; however, it is important to build in the reflective cycle right from the beginning. A culture of continuous learning and improvement cannot be sustained without serious effort. The effort of the enthusiastic beginning can dwindle without a framework of reflective action to keep the cycle going.

In this chapter, principals are provided with a visual representation of the cycle of reflection and action. This cycle should be viewed as a spiral, with the results of the school improvement efforts in the PLC growing each time the cycle is repeated. The five Rs of the cycle represent essential actions of sustainability in a PLC culture: reflect, review data, refocus, revise, and renew.

Within the context of a PLC, the principal and staff reflect regularly on its progress in improving student achievement. Student achievement data are reviewed not just once but at several points in the school year. Decisions are made on instructional practice that refocus the effort to engage students in learning so as to increase their opportunities for success. Data are analyzed, goals are adapted in response to the findings, and plans are revised as necessary to meet the goals. Finally, the commitment that drives teaching and learning at all levels of the school is renewed by the energy generated by the cycle of reflection and action.

The PLC Edifice is capped by the flag of celebration. Recognizing the accomplishments of everyone in the school as they contribute to developing and sustaining a PLC is an important role of the principal. The synergy of collaboration creates a powerful force for action throughout the building phase of creating a PLC. Celebration along the way is also an essential source of fuel to power the cycle of reflection and action that sustains and enhances the collaborative culture.

The Principal's Toolkit

Professional Development Modules

LAYING THE FOUNDATIONS OF MISSION, VISION, VALUES, AND GOALS

In this Professional Development (PD) module, school leaders should adapt strategies and activities to suit individual school contexts. The suggested time to deliver this module is two hours; however, it can easily be broken into shorter segments. Each activity has a suggested time as a guideline. Make any adjustments to content and time that are suitable. The suggested scripts for each activity are easily adapted to school context as well.

1. Think, Pair, Share: Place Mat Activity

(Suggested time: 15 minutes)

Start the PD module with an activity that asks teachers about an experience that illustrates the value of teamwork. Use the graphic organizer in Figure PD1.1 as a tool for accessing prior knowledge. (A full-page template can be found on page 113.)

Use the Place Mat Activity to facilitate a think, pair, share experience. This activity is designed to access prior knowledge and stimulate discussion. Because it is completed in groups of four, it reinforces the value of cooperative learning.

67

Figure PD1.1   Place Mat

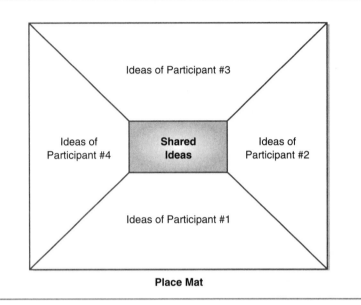

- Create the Place Mat on poster-size paper or chart paper and provide markers for each participant.
- Organize the staff into tables of four so each participant has a quadrant of the Place Mat to write on.
- Review the directions below for completing the Place Mat activity.
- Have participants brainstorm a topic related to the attributes of a PLC school.

Sample Topic: *Think of a time you were a member of an effective group that accomplished its goals. List the characteristics of that group.* This example is designed to focus attention on the importance of collaborative teamwork.

- Here is an example of instructions to participants:
  - ○ Arrange yourselves in groups of four around the Place Mat.
  - ○ *Think:* Each of you will use a quadrant of the Place Mat to record your ideas on the topic. This is an individual

activity done without consultation with others at the table. You will have about three minutes for this activity.

o *Pair:* Now share your list with a partner at the table. You have three minutes.

o *Share at the table:* Next, share with the whole group. Highlight in some way the characteristics that were repeated most often and write these ideas in the center of the place mat. You have five minutes.

o *Share with the room:* Choose a reporter to share with the rest of the staff. We are now going to ask each group to share one or two of the ideas from the center of their place mats.

• As participants respond, record the key ideas. By tapping into the prior knowledge of participants and then validating it by recording it, the value of collaborative teamwork is highlighted.

2. The PLC Edifice: Analogy Activity

(Suggested time: 10 minutes)

Learning is enhanced when analogies are explored. The metaphor of building a PLC emphasizes the collaborative action that it takes to make a PLC possible. The graphic representation of the attributes of a PLC and the corresponding parts of a grand edifice help the staff to grasp the PLC concept (see Figure PD1.2).

• Provide participants with a letter-size or poster-size copy of the building. (A full-page template can be found on page 108.) There are several ways to use a copy of the PLC Edifice graphic. School leaders/teachers can jot down their ideas on the copy. Also, when introducing PLCs, the graphic can be used as an advance organizer, with the model of a building providing an overview of the contents of Chapters 4 and 5.

• Introduce the PLC analogy by using an excerpt from Chapter 1:

School leaders and teachers assume the roles of architect, building contractor, co-owner, and renovator as they create a professional learning community in their schools. The PLC Edifice represents the planning, building, inhabitation, renovation, and enjoyment of a

Figure PD 1.2   PLC Edifice

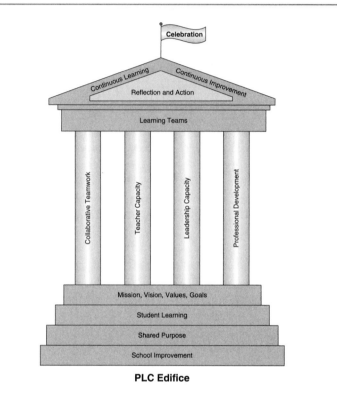

PLC Edifice

professional learning community. School leaders and teachers begin their work as they collaboratively plan and create the foundation of their PLC with student learning and shared purpose. They can then construct the four pillars of collaborative teamwork, teacher capacity, leadership capacity, and professional development to support the school's learning teams. Finally, the PLC Edifice is capped with a commitment to continuous learning and includes reflection and action and results renovations. The flag of celebration completes the metaphorical building process.

- Chapter 1 makes some further correlations between the attributes of a PLC and the structure of a building. Adapt what works.

- To develop the analogy of building a professional learning community, ask questions such as these:
  o How are school leaders like architects?
  o How does a school build a professional learning community?
  o How are we all owners of this new building?
  o Why does the PLC Edifice need four pillars?
  o Why are learning teams so important to holding up the structure of a professional learning community?
  o How does continuous learning protect the school from stormy weather?
  o What flags should we be waving at our school?

3. PLC Learning Grid

(Suggested time: 5 minutes)

- Introduce the use of the PLC Learning Grid. A full-page template to copy can be found on page 111. Some principals may have become familiar with its use for their own learning in Chapter 3. Provide copies and explain to the staff that the PLC Learning Grid is a note-taking tool that can assist them in recording significant ideas and strategies for the study and development of a PLC. In the first two columns, teachers can jot down key ideas and the strategies that emerge from the PD Module. The most important column is the last one—"Ways I Can Use . . ." It provides the opportunity to move from theory to practice by asking teachers to make connections to their own school context. Most of all, the PLC Learning Grid is designed to answer this question: How can we use what we have learned about PLCs to improve student achievement?
- Model the use of the PLC Learning Grid by filling out the beginning of the Grid with staff. Develop brief notes from the PLC Edifice analogy activity.

4. The Foundation Attributes of a PLC: Knowledge-Sharing Jigsaw Activity

(Suggested Time: 30 minutes)

The PLC Edifice helps to give the overall picture of what it takes to be a PLC. It's like a table of contents for Chapters 4, 5, and 6.

The focus for this module is laying the foundations of a PLC by discussing the shared purpose of student learning and then collaboratively developing statements of the mission, vision, values, and goals that will lead to action. Principals can use several approaches to help staff become knowledgeable about the foundations of a PLC:

- Develop a PowerPoint slide show or overhead presentation based on the material on mission, vision, values, and goals at the beginning of this chapter and in Chapter 1.
- Use print excerpts from this handbook.
- Search the Internet for articles on PLCs. Most of the well-known researchers in the field have articles from journals posted on easily accessible sites. Provoke discussion by providing articles from educational journals and Web sites. Articles are a valuable resource of current thought on PLCs and provide interesting starting points for discussion.
- Use excerpts about mission, vision, values, and goals from books by PLC experts. Choose four excerpts to develop and facilitate in a jigsaw activity.

  1. Number each excerpt from 1 to 4.

  2. Put the participants in groups of four, called the Home Groups. Number off the members of all the groups from 1 to 4; each member is responsible for reading the excerpt that corresponds to that number. Ensure silence while all the participants read. Therefore, one participant is reading about mission, one about vision, one about values, and one about goals.

  3. After reading time, have the participants move into Expert Groups, where all the members have read the same excerpt. For example, all those who have read about mission are together as Expert Group 1, and so on.

  4. Instruct each expert group to develop a short presentation summarizing the key ideas of the assigned excerpt for their Home Groups or for the whole group. Chart paper, overhead sheets, or note paper can be provided. The task for the goals excerpt might be worded like this: *As experts, be prepared to share the key ideas of your excerpt*

on goals. How can the ideas of the assigned excerpt be used to help to develop goals in our school?

- A short session introducing the foundation attributes of *mission, vision, values,* and *goals* helps staff to clarify the meaning of these familiar terms in relation to PLCs. The focus here is defining the terms to facilitate the following activity, developing statements of mission, vision, values, and goals.

5. Mission, Vision, Values, Goals: Fishbone Activity

(Suggested time: 60 minutes)

After introducing the staff to the key ideas associated with developing the mission, vision, values, and goals of a PLC, it's time to lay the foundation. The cornerstone is collaborative action. Mission, vision, and values statements must be developed and goals articulated at this initiation stage. Most principals are familiar with a process for doing this and may want to stick to the familiar. What would be different this time is that the context of creating a PLC infuses the process.

However, principals and/or the PLC Steering Team may find the graphic organizer in Figure PD1.3 useful to facilitate laying the foundations of their PLC—the Fishbone.

The Fishbone Planning Template offers a visual representation of the four elements of the PLC foundation. Mission, vision, and values are the topics of the top fins. Space to develop three goals is given in the bottom three fins. The idea is to use the Fishbone Template as a method of collaboratively brainstorming the content of the school's mission, vision, values, and goals. After collecting the ideas expressed on the Fishbone Template, the actual statements of mission, vision, values, and goals can be constructed in sentences. Principals and/or the PLC Steering Team can design their own method of using the Fishbone activity or use the following variation of the process:

1. Create the Fishbone Template in various sizes. (A full-page template can be found on page 114.) Print a letter-size template for each staff member, one poster-size template for each group, and one master Fishbone Template that the

Figure PD 1.3   The Fishbone

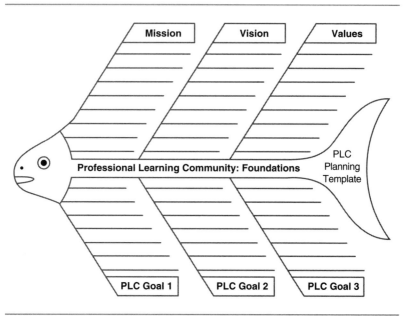

whole staff can view at a meeting. The master Fishbone could also be reproduced as a slide on an overhead or an electronic file on a computer screen. In both cases, responses from the staff should be recorded and projected so all the staff can see the template.

2. Have participants in their groups brainstorm ideas that should be in the school's mission, vision, and values statements. Have them place these ideas on the bones of the fish skeleton in the top three fins.

3. Have each group report their ideas for each fin. Have each group do all the points for *mission* first. From all the reports, narrow the key ideas down to a few and record them on the master Fishbone Template. Then move on to the next foundation of *vision* and repeat the exercise. Finally, focus on *values*.

4. Once the bones of the top fin are filled, have each group go back to their Fishbone Template and brainstorm the elements of three goals for building a PLC that will use

collaborative action to improve student achievement. Repeat the full staff discussion, focusing on narrowing the number of goals down to three. Place the key ideas for three goals on the skeleton in the bottom fins.

5. Have the PLC Steering Team take the master Fishbone and compose a draft of the mission, vision, values, and goals statements. The draft would then be made available to staff for feedback.

6. Share the final version of the mission, vision, values, and goals statements at the next staff meeting. These are your foundations for the next stage of building learning teams. Make this an opportunity for celebration together.

Here is a possible script that can be used by the facilitators:

- Arrange yourselves in groups of four around the Fishbone Template.
- Think about the key ideas you would want expressed in the school's mission, vision, and values statements if we are to be a PLC. Making use of the top three fins of mission, vision, and values, brainstorm several important elements that you would like to see in each of these foundations of a PLC. When the groups are finished, each group will report to the staff as a whole, and we'll use this master Fishbone Template to capture the points that resonate with you the most. (After about 15 minutes, lead a discussion of another 15 minutes that gathers their ideas from the group-sized Fishbone Templates and places those most frequently mentioned on the master Fishbone Template.)
- Now that we have collected what we want to see in our mission, vision, and values statements, let's create the goals that will propel us into action as a PLC. In your groups, brainstorm the elements of three goals and place your ideas on the skeleton of the three bottom fins. Following this, each group will share their ideas with the whole staff, and once again we will record your ideas on the master Fishbone Template. (After about 15 minutes, lead a discussion of another 15 minutes that gathers their ideas from the group-sized Fishbone Templates and places

those most frequently mentioned on the master Fishbone Template.)

- The PLC Steering Team will work with your input and draft mission, vision, values, and goals statements. We will ask for your feedback on this and present a final version at our next staff meeting.

Going through a collaborative activity that lays the foundation of a PLC is extremely important to the establishment of a culture of collaborative action in the school. It doesn't have to take too long. Most educators have participated in creating mission, vision, values, and goals statements at some point in their careers. What is important here is the focus on the shared purpose of student learning and a commitment to school improvement. Keeping the brainstorming activity to about an hour sets a productive pace. The PLC Steering Team can then take away the staff contributions and craft the actual statements. Design a feedback process on the draft statements and then finalize them.

PROFESSIONAL DEVELOPMENT MODULE 2

PLC PORTFOLIO AND PLC SNAPSHOT ASSESSMENT

(FOR FOLLOW-UP STAFF MEETING)

(Suggested time: 60 minutes)

Follow-Up Staff Meeting: PLC Foundations and the PLC Portfolio and PLC Snapshot Assessment

- *Celebration:* Use the opportunity of the next staff meeting to celebrate the development of the new mission, vision, values, and goals statements. Have the statements printed or presented in an attractive format. Provide special refreshments and highlight the contributions of the PLC Steering Team. Design an activity that has fun with the statements if the staff is open to this. Perhaps a poem, song, or rap could be composed and performed.
- *PLC Portfolio:* This may be the occasion to introduce the PLC Portfolio described in Chapter 3. By ceremoniously placing the mission, vision, values, and goals statements in the PLC Portfolio, the principal signals the importance of the process to the whole school and indicates that the building of the PLC has begun. More will follow and be celebrated. The PLC Portfolio can be shared with students and parents as the school transforms itself into a PLC.
- *PLC Snapshot Assessment:* The PLC Snapshot Assessment can also be introduced at this staff meeting. This tool sets the tone of accountability and allows the staff to see that progress is already being made in the first indicators of building a PLC. Both the PLC Snapshot Assessment and PLC Portfolio remind the school that building a PLC is a long-term goal with many stages along the way. It will take several years of commitment to develop and put in place a culture that sustains the attributes of a PLC.

PROFESSIONAL DEVELOPMENT MODULE 3

PLC LEARNING TEAMS

This introduction to learning teams could be facilitated by the principal or the school PLC Steering Team. In keeping with the other PD Modules, principals will adapt strategies and activities to suit individual school contexts. The suggested length of time to deliver the module is 2 hours; however, it can easily be broken into shorter segments.

1. Introduction to Collaborative Teamwork: *Finding Nemo* Movie Excerpt Activity

(Suggested time: 15 minutes)

Using a video excerpt from a movie is one strategy to capture interest, illustrate concepts, and start a focused discussion. With this activity, a short excerpt from a film is used to create an analogy that focuses on the collaborative teamwork attribute of a PLC. Show a three-minute video clip from *Finding Nemo* or another film that has a positive teamwork segment. In *Finding Nemo*, there is a three-minute segment near the end where fish are caught in the net and they must coordinate their actions to escape. After viewing the segment, ask staff to have a short discussion in small groups: What lesson is presented in this film segment? In what ways do we collaborate in our school? After five minutes, invite each group to share their ideas with the whole group. This leads to a discussion of collaboration to achieve a goal. The analogy can be used to expand participant understanding of the learning teams, leadership skills, and collaborative skills.

2. Introduction to the PLC Grid

This activity is used to introduce the PLC Grid if it has not been introduced in the Planning for PLCs module in Chapter 4, or it can be used as a reminder to participants to record their reflections on the module as they go along.

The PLC Learning Grid that appears in the Principal's Toolkit: Reproducibles can be photocopied for workshop participants. It is a tool to record the content and strategies presented in this PD

Module. Most of all, the PLC Grid is designed to answer this question: How can we use what we have learned about PLC learning teams to improve student achievement?

3. Introduction to Learning Teams and the Four Pillars

(Suggested time: 15 minutes)
Choose a method of sharing the attributes of learning teams in a PLC: collaborative teamwork, teacher capacity, leadership capacity, and professional development. Possible methods include the following:

- *PLC Edifice analogy activity:* Review the graphic organizer from Chapter 4, placing an emphasis on the four pillars that support learning teams.
- *Slideshow:* Create a short slide presentation based on the material in this handbook. Both Chapter 1 and Chapter 5 offer information on learning teams and the four pillars that support them.
- *Discussion:* Copy excerpts from this handbook and use them as starting points for a discussion on planning for the development of PLC learning teams.

The facilitator(s) should keep this review of the attributes short and plan to return to it at a follow-up meeting.

4. Learning From Case Studies: Jigsaw Activity

(Suggested time: 60 minutes)
The purpose of this jigsaw activity is for the staff to share knowledge in a collaborative manner. The four case studies for this jigsaw are found later in the Principal's Toolkit: "Leading and Learning in Teams in an Elementary School," "Implementing a Professional Learning Community in a Secondary School," "Learning Teams in an Elementary School," and "One School's Journey: SMART Goals for Student Success in a Middle School." All were written by school administrators who implemented PLC learning teams in their schools. These case studies outline the steps the principals used to develop learning teams in their

schools, including memos, and describe some of the results of the work of the learning teams.

How to run a jigsaw:

1. Number the case studies from 1 to 4.

2. Put the participants in groups of four, called the Home Groups. Number off the members of all the groups from 1 to 4; each is responsible for reading the case study that corresponds to the number. Ensure silence while all the participants read.

3. After reading time, have the participants move into Expert Groups, where all the members have read the same case study. For example, all those who have read Case Study 1 are together in Expert Group 1.

4. Instruct each expert group to develop a short presentation summarizing the key ideas of the assigned case study for their Home Groups or for the whole group. Chart paper, over-head sheets, or note paper can be provided. The task might be worded like this: *As experts, be prepared to share the key ideas of your case study. How can the ideas of the assigned case study be used to help to build collaborative teams in our school?*

Alternate Sources of Materials for Jigsaw Activity

There are several alternate sources of articles or short excerpts for a jigsaw activity on learning teams. The facilitator chooses and distributes four short articles or excerpts from a book on the role of learning teams in a PLC, such as the book edited by DuFour, Eaker, and DuFour (2005), *On Common Ground: The Power of Professional Learning Communities.* The Internet is also an excellent source of articles. Just type in key words such as *professional learning community* and *learning teams.* Professional journals, such as *Educational Leadership* (ASCD) and *Phi Delta Kappan,* likewise offer a number of articles on the topic in past issues.

5. Collaborative Action:
Establishing PLC Learning Teams

(Suggested time: 30 minutes)

The principal or PLC Steering Team facilitates a discussion of what comes next in developing the school as a PLC. The activity with the case studies allows the principal and staff to apply what they have learned to their own context. Teachers have the opportunity to say, "This will work in our school," or, "No, that's not for us." The facilitator could adapt several questions from the set of "Guiding Questions" that follows the PD Module to help in this process of developing the school norms for working in learning teams to raise student achievement. The norms of operating in learning teams are developed together and recorded in draft form. This draft will become part of the PLC implementation plan. Allow several weeks for reflection and include teachers in the process of finalizing the PLC implementation plan.

This PD Module, "PLC Learning Teams," can be adapted to suit your needs. This process of collaborating to create the organizational structure that will support learning teams in a PLC is very important. The process of developing the school implementation plan will not be easy. The school will build its collaborative culture over time. Starting out by modeling a collaborative approach to planning from the beginning helps the principal and staff to understand both the successes and challenges that go with work of this nature.

The Principal's Toolkit

Case Studies

This collection of case studies, written by principals and vice principals about their experiences in implementing and leading PLCs, is a valuable resource for school leaders. The administrators have provided not only a description of what happened in several Ontario, Canada, schools but also the templates of the memos and forms they used in the process of leading a PLC. Case studies for both elementary and secondary schools are included. Case Studies 1 to 4 could be used in the Professional Development Module in Chapter 5, "PLC Learning Teams," as the four readings of the Jigsaw Activity. Case Study 5 describes the process of establishing a learning team for school leaders within a district.

CASE STUDY 1: LEADING AND LEARNING IN TEAMS IN A NEW ELEMENTARY SCHOOL

by Steve McCombe, Principal

This elementary school was formed as a new school as a result of an amalgamation of two schools in the district in September of 2004. For the principal, the challenge was how to form a professional learning community while bringing together two school communities to form a new school. The principal had a vision of the new school as a learning organization that would bring together interested, willing people to create a shared vision, with trust and understanding as a foundation, to nurture continuous learning.

The advantage of creating a new school was that the administration could establish with staff, prior to the first school year, the goals needed to form a new learning community. Although they would adopt certain practices and routines from both schools, they were going to form something new. From January to June of the first year, joint planning and professional learning sessions were held with the staffs from both schools. They engaged in professional dialogue so that staff would know what a professional learning community was and what the expectations would be for teachers within such an environment. It was made explicit that the staff would be engaged in shared decision making, a shared mission and vision, addressing student learning with mutually coordinated professional learning, and using collaborative planning time as a means to get there.

The principal sought to get the right people in place at the school as the administrative team worked through the staffing process in the spring. Staffs from both schools were encouraged to decide if the challenge of forming a new professional learning community was something they wanted to engage in or whether they would prefer to seek a new challenge at another school. Most staff from the forming partners decided to work at the new school. During the staffing process for available positions, the principal and vice principal spent the first part of the hiring interview outlining explicitly the direction the new school would take to become a professional learning community. Those who were interviewed were informed that if they were the successful candidates, they would need to work with other staff to help form a professional learning community.

School leaders learned that there are certainly no stepwise rules that automatically lead to the creation of a successful learning community in a school. Part of the challenge was to determine what needed to be done and when. The principal felt that he needed to model and foster an atmosphere of trust with the staff and community as they developed their learning community to focus on improving student learning. One of the ways to accomplish this was through establishing collaborative teams of teachers. The beginning of the school year was anything but typical. The staff met for two days in August, prior to the beginning of school, to begin planning for the school year. The staff was unable to rely on past practice because new routines and procedures had to be put into place. Together, they established the new routines in the emerging professional learning community.

Division leaders for the primary, junior, and intermediate divisions had been chosen by staff the previous June. In September, the principal met with the division leaders to discuss how they would begin to proceed in addressing the school's mission, vision, values, and goals. During an early-dismissal day early in the fall, one of the division leaders led staff through what a professional learning community looked like and what the implications were for the school. Time was then given to each division to begin planning how to address student learning as a division. Some collaborative time was also created during class time for staff to plan together. For the principal, it was refreshing to watch how the staff at the newly amalgamated school worked together to begin forming their learning community.

As a staff, they tried to focus on drafting a mission statement during the fall. If they were to be truly effective in working collaboratively on student learning, they would need to have a mission that would guide their efforts. The staff were asked ahead of time to do readings about developing a mission statement. In the division leaders' meetings, they discussed how they would go about getting to the mission. The assistance of the division leaders was very helpful in the timing of putting the mission statement on the agenda for staff. A mission statement is not a process that can be accomplished in a few easy steps, they discovered. It took several attempts. If staff are to buy into what the mission is saying and if it is to act as a guide for the school, it seems that allowing time and staff input is a good thing for it to become a meaningful statement. This process cannot be rushed.

As the fall moved along, the staff began to focus on their school improvement goal. A committee reviewed student data from both forming schools, such as standardized test results, Developmental Reading Assessment, and other available test scores, to pinpoint an area of focus for the school goal. The staff understood that the goal was to be a SMART (specific, measurable, attainable, realistic, time-bound) goal. The input of staff was invaluable as we worked through this process. Collaborative time was then established for each division to begin to address student learning and to focus on the school goal. The staff used their division leaders' meetings to begin to establish the focus, and then every two weeks, divisions were to meet during class time to plan. Collaborative time was made possible by the principal, vice principal, and nonteaching staff working with students in the gym on the monthly behavior focus. Collaborative time was a priority, and the staff were asked to plan learning activities during this time.

As division teams met, each division leader was asked to complete a Team Feedback Form and give it to the principal at the completion of the meeting. The feedback form was a method to help the divisions focus on particular areas of student learning that needed to be addressed. The collaborative groups got right to work identifying group norms describing what was expected of group members during collaborative meetings, long-range planning of instruction, looking at student data, addressing student reading, engaging in professional learning, and involving parents. Divisions also decided where and how their collaborative meetings would be set up, indicating that they would be meeting biweekly as a whole group or in pairs with a grade partner during another session.

Professional learning for staff was actively encouraged. Staff meeting time was used to focus on professional development rather than information that could be presented on paper. A study group was formed where teachers met weekly or biweekly at lunchtime to study a book of their choosing for professional learning. The book was purchased for them to keep, and a light lunch was provided. The school chose to make participation in the study groups optional, with the hope that the momentum with staff would build on its own.

The learning community at this elementary school is still young and has many challenges ahead. However, it is very rewarding to see what can happen when a group of professionals work together to address student learning. The journey may seem long and in many ways challenging; it begins with the first step.

Practical Thoughts for Establishing Effective Collaborative Teams

- Develop trust with staff—you won't be successful without it.
- Think big, start small.
- Make intentions explicit with staff—collaboration by invitation doesn't work.
- Talk it up—plant the seeds with key staff, have informal discussions in the halls, etc.

- Use staff meeting time, early dismissal days, and PD days to discuss what a professional learning community does; what successful collaborative teams look like and do; and what collegiality is and its impact on the success of a professional learning community, especially the collaborative teams.
- Use articles to "jigsaw" in a staff meeting to help staff understand what research says about professional learning communities.
- Discuss what collaborative teams should focus on.
- Identify leaders—establish division leaders (elementary) and department heads (secondary) and have them assist with the process of setting up collaborative teams.
- Establish priorities—schedule collaborative time and keep it sacred (e.g., don't schedule field trips or guest speakers when collaborative time is scheduled).
- Establish norms for teams (e.g., How should each member behave?).
- Establish a focus for each meeting (e.g., the meeting is about student learning; it is not a collective "complaining" session).
- Expect accountability—the leader or other team member writes what was accomplished in the meeting using a TEAM feedback form and gives it to the principal.
- Respond to the TEAM feedback form.
- Reflect—constantly talk with staff about what is working and their concerns.
- Provide collaborative planning time for staff regularly.

Reflecting on the Process

- The principal is the key person in establishing and keeping the ship on course.
- Work with the teacher leaders to help establish direction and value their input.
- Talk, talk, and talk the vision.
- Stay involved with the process.
- Participate if possible in collaborative planning sessions.
- Respond to TEAM feedback sheet.
- Believe that it can be done!

A Memo to the Staff From the Principal: A Professional Learning Community

The following memo was sent to the staff at the start of the initiative. The principal based the approach on the DuFour and Eaker model (1998). The memo provided written guidance and outlined how the school was to approach the creation of a learning community.

The following format is something to read and think about as we move toward becoming a professional learning community. There is no such thing as three easy steps in this process. A true PLC only comes about when a collegial staff works collaboratively to address student learning. These things cannot be forced or mandated, but the professional literature is clear on the benefits for students and their learning when a school is able to become a learning community. The following is intended to act as a guide as we move through the process together.

Six Characteristics of a Learning Community (DuFour & Eaker, 1998)

1. Shared mission, vision, values, goals
2. Collaborative teams
3. Collective inquiry
4. Action orientation/experimentation
5. Commitment to continuous improvement
6. Results orientation

Clarity of Purpose
- Our purpose is student learning.
- We need to establish SMART goals.

Underlying Assumptions
- The focus is on learning, not teaching.
- We can make a difference.
- Our school can be more effective.
- All students can learn.
- When students don't learn, we will have a uniform response to this.
- We are here to see that all students can learn.
- We can work together as a team to help students learn.
- Everyone is on the team.
- The focus of the team is learning.

- There are expectations of team members and how they contribute to the team.
- Collaborative team sessions will have a focus, and feedback will be submitted at the end of the meeting.
- People improvement is the key to school improvement.
- Significant school improvement will impact teaching and learning.

The Critical Questions

It is essential that we are clear about our vision and what we hope to accomplish as a school. Best practice must drive our vision. Our school goal needs to be written in a way that we are able to know whether we are achieving our purpose.

- What is it we expect students to learn?
- How will we know they have learned it?
- How will we respond when they don't learn?

Value/Vision Statement

We need to state the good intentions of our mission statement/vision in collective commitments that describe what each member of the school is prepared to do to help make the vision a reality.

To achieve our Mission Statement in the area of curriculum, it must address these questions:

- What will we do to "enable our students to reach their full potential"?
- Are we clear about what we want to accomplish as a school?
- Is it short enough that we can articulate it?

In 2004/2005, we identified the following statement after much discussion and reflection:

Helping students develop their full potential is a safe and supportive learning environment.

Our Value/Vision Statement

Based on the above, what are we going to do to help students achieve our mission?

The School Goal

What will our instructional focus be this year?

Question 1: What do we expect our students to learn?

- **Using data to drive the process** (e.g., What do our data tell us about what our students need in reading?): This addresses a specific area of student learning need based on our data.
- **Identify a SMART goal:** **S**pecific and strategic, **M**easurable, **A**ttainable, **R**esults oriented, **T**ime Bound

Question 2: How will we know they have learned it?

Assessment drives the whole process. Part of our professional learning focus this year will be on how we assess student learning.

- What will we use to determine if students are successful? (Assessment tools?)
- Are we using formative as well as summative assessment?
- What tools of assessment should be used by all of us?
- How are we using assessment to drive instruction?
- Are we being successful with instruction, and how do we know for sure?
- How often do we communicate progress to parents?

Question 3: What will be our response when they don't learn it?

- How are we going to improve every student's achievement?
- What is our approach to the reluctant learner?

Team Feedback Sheet

Team:	
Date:	
Team Members Present and Regrets:	
PLC Goal for Meeting:	
Next Steps:	
Team Responsibilities and Time Line:	
Administrator Review:	
Date:	

CASE STUDY 2: IMPLEMENTING A PROFESSIONAL LEARNING COMMUNITY IN A SECONDARY SCHOOL

by Brian Serafini, Vice Principal

Background

The district consists of 11 secondary schools. The implementation of professional learning communities was a districtwide initiative. A districtwide steering committee consisting of both elementary and secondary personnel and superintendents was formed to help develop and oversee implementation within the schools.

Professional Learning Community Steering Committee

The PLC steering committee created three tenets for the implementation of the districtwide implementation process: We, not I; Do less, better; and Success for All. Each tenet was based on DuFour and Eaker's PLC model (1998). The steering committee also created a tight/loose leadership list that was to be followed when implementing PLCs in the school. Finally, the committee assisted in getting district support for the project. The first year would be a year of awareness; the next year, the year of implementation; and subsequent years would consist of sustainability, reflection, and improvement. As well, at the district annual Principal/Vice Principal Conference, both secondary and elementary administrators had the opportunity to receive training on professional learning communities. Print and electronic resources were made available. Financial support allowed district administrators and members of the steering committee to travel to Adlai Stevenson High School, Richard DuFour's former high school. The purpose of the excursion was to observe firsthand the practical aspects of DuFour's professional learning community. The team was given the opportunity to observe meetings of their learning teams, to talk with teachers and students at the school, and to explore the structures created within the school to help sustain a learning community.

Implementing a Professional Learning Community

The case school is a secondary school consisting of 1,750 students and over 100 staff members. Many of the staff members have been at the school for most of their teaching careers, and only recently has the school begun to experience an influx of younger professionals. The question that challenged the administration was how to introduce the concept of professional learning communities to the staff. The approach decided upon was to focus on the third tenet created by the steering committee—Success for All. We wanted to reorient the school from a teaching institution into a learning institution.

An early initiative with the staff was to send some of the teachers to Adlai Stevenson High School so that they could also experience a professional learning community firsthand. Once volunteers came forward, they were supplied with short readings outlining the theory behind professional learning communities, as well as research outlining the integral role of the principles of professional learning communities in improving student success. The trip helped the staff members begin to understand the daily operations of a professional learning community. A second group of interested staff members was sent and upon their return, a Student Success Team of teachers and two vice principals was formed. From then on, professional learning community initiatives at the school level was the responsibility of this team, thus avoiding the top-down model of implementation and modeling the collaborative approach to implementation.

Feedback from the Student Success Team was instrumental in procuring the services of a training consultant to further the staff's understanding of professional learning communities, learning, and student success. The Student Success Team asked the trainer to focus on the three fundamental questions of a professional learning community: What do we want them to learn? How do we know if they have learned it? What do we do if they haven't? We hoped teachers would understand how, as a staff, they held within them the expertise and knowledge to ensure that all students can succeed. The trainer's approach was what the staff needed. Most were intrigued by the concept, and this facilitated the work of our Student Success Team and the administration team.

The School Success Team worked to develop an effective format for subject departments to implement the qualities of a professional learning community. This evolved, and department heads became the school's Directions Team. The heads worked in conjunction with the administration team in overseeing professional learning community implementation. The Directions Team received inservice from the district on a variety of topics pertaining to professional learning communities and student success; as well, the Student Success Team reported directly to the Directions Team.

At the same time, a joint initiative of representatives from the administration, Student Success Team, and Directions Team created a Pyramid of Intervention Strategies (DuFour, 2004) specific to their school. In conjunction with this, the typical meetings concerning "at-risk" students took on an enhanced format. Once a month, members of the administration team; the school's attendance, drug, and alcohol counselors; along with the heads of guidance and special education, the school's "at-risk" coordinator, and the district psychologist meet to discuss individual students, the services they are receiving, and the success or lack of success they are experiencing.

Most recently, the school's Student Success Team has created a new schedule for the coming year that would reduce the lunch period from two periods to a common lunch. The purpose of this new schedule is to allow for adequate supervision time so that a late assignment room could be established. Teachers would assign students to the room during each lunch period until the assignment was completed.

The next hurdle for the Student Success Team was to create a model of release time during the school day for our learning teams to meet. Currently the team is working on a model that would see a five-period day consisting of 60-minute periods instead of the current four 76-minute periods. The shorter periods will allow for learning teams to meet for one hour once every two weeks. This time is an essential component if the learning teams are going to achieve the district's tenet: Success for All.

CASE STUDY 3: LEARNING TEAMS: AN ELEMENTARY SCHOOL

by Cindy Harris, Principal

This case study elementary school is a K–6 school serving a rural community.

The principal began with the belief that all students could be successful. She believed that each staff member was a learner; she considered herself the lead learner. She believed that each staff member was a leader. She believed that staff needed to build toward a collaborative process where they worked toward the success for all students.

After almost two years of building a mutual, trusting relationship, where communication and support were key elements, the principal introduced articles to the staff about professional learning communities using a jigsaw approach. A common theme that arose was the issue around needing time. Staff indicated that they were now resource-rich. They wanted and needed time to use resources to meet the expectations of language, math, and assessment initiatives that would improve student learning.

After participating in a District Assessment Training Institute, where resources such as *The Learning Team Guide* were shared, the principal developed a proposal with staff about learning teams, defining and providing a rationale for them. The proposal, a three-year plan, challenged the way the school had done business in the past. It also required a school budget commitment, supporting human resources rather than material resources. An outline of the first two years of the plan appears below.

Year 1

Staff Memo From Principal

Learning Teams Proposal

Rationale: Why Learning Teams? A learning team is not simply a group of individuals who get together periodically to talk about what is happening. Nor is it a book club that gathers to discuss what an author said. Rather, it is a small group of professionals who agree to experiment with new ideas and meet regularly for a specific period of time to share specific professional growth experience guided by specific goals and purposes.

Learning team meetings are times for sharing lessons learned in the classroom, not those just derived from reading a book; it is a time to share successes and discuss strategies that worked, as well as share difficulties, determine why they arose, and find solutions. A learning team provides a forum for learning, planning, testing ideas, and reflecting together.

Professional Learning Community Plan

Year 1

- One half-day monthly will be provided to allow each division to meet. Literacy will be the main focus.
- Any division issues will be addressed at this meeting. Time needs to be limited for operational issues (30 minutes at end of meeting). An agenda will be developed by the facilitator, in conjunction with the principal.
- There will be no division meetings on Wednesdays. Instead, our school will be made up of three teams, an Assessment Learning Team, a Math Learning Team, and a Literacy Learning Team. There will be a School Direction Team consisting of the literacy contact teacher, the math contact teacher, the learning resource teacher, and the principal.
- Each of the three learning teams (Assessment, Math, and Literacy) should consist of no more than six members. Each staff member will be a member of one of the teams. This does not limit any teacher from being a member of more than one learning team. Each team will require representation across the divisions. Each team will be facilitated by the literacy contact teacher, the math contact teacher, the learning resource teacher, or the principal.
- Teams will meet monthly, with an agenda. All minutes will be posted to the school Web site, in a folder specific to that team, accessible by all staff members.
- Teacher support reading materials for the teams will be provided. The Literacy Team already has reading material from which to choose.
- Each team's mandate will be to improve student learning, demonstrate how improvement was achieved (or what difficulties still remain), and provide data to support the information. Each team will develop a measurable goal and build expectations as part of the school program plan.
- Teams will be required to share their information throughout the year with the other teachers on staff. Literacy will be the focus at the Division Team meetings, assessment will be the focus on early closing days, and math will be the focus on staff meeting days.
- The School Direction Team will meet three times during the first year to identify and resolve issues and clarify common directions for the teams.

At the end of the first year, all staff agreed that they would continue with Year 2. Ideas on changes came as a result of feedback given by staff.

Year 2

Division PLC Teams

- Meet one half-day monthly (Monday).
- Meet one Wednesday after school. Other meetings will be determined by the grade level or division team.
- Develop an agenda for each meeting. The first part of the meeting will be devoted to full division initiatives, both language and math. Teams will then move into grade-level teams. A limited amount of time will be devoted to operational issues. Minutes must be posted to the school Web site.
- Develop SMART goals in language, math, and assessment.
- Develop norms of collaborative teamwork.
- Use a feedback sheet each meeting to identify actions and next steps.

Grade-Level Teams

- Develop grade-specific goals, identifying a current state and the desired state.
- Develop a common set of expectations for language and math, with common assessment strategies at a common time (e.g., currently using reading assessments each term).
- Focus on reading, writing (communication), and mathematics (problem solving and numeracy).
- Develop one "design down" module, including assessment and evaluation each term.
- Develop an overall School Assessment Plan, including grade-specific and board-directed assessments.
- Develop common homework expectations and strategies.
- Use the Education Quality and Accountability Office (EQAO) model of questions in language and math throughout the planning of units.
- Use a feedback sheet each meeting to identify actions and next steps.
- Use these three key questions to drive the work of the learning communities: What do we want each student to learn? How will we know when each student has learned it? How will we respond when a student experiences difficulty in learning?

School Direction PLC Team

- Members include primary literacy contact teacher, junior literacy contact teacher, primary math contact teacher, junior math contact teacher, learning resource teacher, and principal.
- Meet one half-day monthly (Thursday) to focus on school program plans, to facilitate team meetings, and to ensure continuity and consistency across divisions.

Results of the Professional Learning Community Initiative

The School Direction PLC Team was invited to be part of a district professional learning community project after Year 1, where the staff had time to explore their purpose further. They developed a specific goal for this team, which has provided a clear focus for what takes place in the Division PLC Team meetings: *Promote and facilitate the collaboration of teachers, linking it to improved student learning.*

At the end of Year 1, School Program Goals for literacy were met across the grades. At the end of Year 2, with the focus on the three key assessment questions, discussion about improved student learning was more directed. Team meetings involved a talk-action-talk process. Processes were used in a classroom and discussed what worked, what didn't, and what to try next. By using criteria that helped reflect on the professional learning community teams in the school, a focus on next steps has been identified.

The principal and staff believe that student improvement occurs when staff experience and model learning. Since sustained school improvement impacts teaching and learning, they believe that as a professional learning community, they will continue to make a difference for staff, students, and the community.

CASE STUDY 4: ONE SCHOOL'S JOURNEY: SMART GOALS FOR STUDENT SUCCESS IN A MIDDLE SCHOOL

by Deborah MacDonald, Principal

This middle school of Grades 6–8 is a diverse, high-performing school serving 940 adolescents. The mission of "Live, Love, Laugh, Learn in Harmony, and Leave a Legacy" inspires students and staff to improve continually. School improvement is not a new concept, and school leaders have been searching for methods to improve their school for decades. Each leader searches for the path to student success for all learners. Much has been written on learning communities and their role in school improvement. The school implemented SMART (Specific, Measurable, Attainable, Results oriented, and Time bound) goals to give the school the organization and framework to be successful (Conzemius & O'Neill, 2002). Its goal-oriented, student-focused approach enabled teachers to work collaboratively toward student improvement. Moreover, SMART goals provided a format and momentum to continue and sustain the improvement.

In 2002, grade-level teams began setting SMART goals in the subject area of literacy, specifically reading. The journey began when the staff attended a one-day workshop presented by Mike Schmoker: "SMART Goals: Results the Essential Element of School Improvement." This professional development activity was the catalyst that began discussions on how the staff would implement SMART goals. A further resource that was utilized was *The Handbook for SMART School Teams* by Conzemius and O'Neill (2002).

From there, the staff began their plan of action. They established a framework with structures and time lines for each team to use to set their SMART goal. Each team was required to set a goal but was free to choose an expectation within the reading domain. Release time for teams to plan and evaluate their SMART goal was provided. Teams planned together to prepare the preassessment, teaching strategies, and the postassessment. At the end of the first year, each team shared their learning, assessment strategies, and results at a staff meeting. Each team accomplished a great deal, and the teachers were very proud of their accomplishments. With every goal, student achievement improved. Teachers could see the effectiveness of their instruction as the results were immediate and instantly gratifying. Staff commitment to the SMART goal process increased over time as they witnessed the impact it was having on student success.

At the end of the first year, teachers reflected on their successes and looked for ways to improve the process. Upon reflection, teachers learned that some of their goals were too large and therefore difficult to assess. As a result, the following year, their goals became more specific. In Year 3, each grade team continued to establish two SMART goals. In addition, the School Success Literacy Team developed a schoolwide goal and a grade-specific continuum to work toward that goal.

SMART goals have been instrumental in improving student achievement. Even in its infancy, it became evident that SMART goals were having a positive effect. Teachers focused on a common goal. Discussions about student learning, teaching strategies, and consistent evaluation dominated their grade-level meetings. Teachers collaborated to reach their SMART goal and became collectively responsible for student learning. New teachers were engaged immediately in ongoing professional dialogue and were given much needed direction on best practices. An essential element for the success was strong grade-level teams who understood the benefits of teamwork and very strong grade-level chairs who were able to lead these teams successfully.

The principal's role was also a key to success. The school principal provided ongoing support and guidance, particularly for the team chairs. Leading by example, engaging in the dialogue, and commitment to the continuous learning process were also important. Trusting the team chairs and empowering them to make decisions built the leadership capacity in the school.

The staff have discovered that the benefits of implementing SMART goals are

- improved student achievement;
- increased teacher collaboration;
- effective teacher experimentation with new teaching strategies; and
- increased teacher leadership.

SMART goals are the organizing tool that has helped the staff to continue to be a true learning organization. As Peter Senge (1990) has said,

The learning organization is "a place" where people continually expand their capacity to create the results they truly desire, where new and expansive patterns of thinking are nurtured, where collective aspiration is set free, and where people are continually learning how to learn together. (p. 3)

CASE STUDY 5: LEARNING TEAMS FOR PRINCIPALS AND VICE PRINCIPALS

by Mary Nanavati and Linda Massey

This case study and proposal template is useful to support the development of principal and vice principal learning teams across a district. By forming their own learning teams, administrators can support each other in developing PLCs in their schools.

The role of the principal/vice principal as a model of a self-directed learner is at the heart of what many educators say is necessary for effective leadership in today's schools. Collaborative learning and leading are essential in a professional learning community. One valuable method of building leadership capacity is for school leaders to create their own learning teams. What is learned as a member of a learning team can create positive change within school communities. The following case study describes how a group of vice principals in a large urban school district created their own learning team and have sustained it.

Secondary Vice Principal Learning Team

"School leaders must show others the importance of professional learning and development. They must continue to learn, inside and outside the school, in order to provide positive change" (Fullan, 2005a, p. 5).

Leaders in collaborative learning teams! One of the most valuable learning strategies for school leaders is to create their own learning teams. Principals and vice principals who develop a supportive learning environment among themselves serve as role models of collective inquiry in their schools and across the school district. The establishment of their own learning teams provides school leaders with the opportunity to be reflective practitioners of their craft of school leadership.

Over the past nine years, a group of secondary vice principals in the district have been meeting together monthly as a learning team. This learning team of secondary vice principals facilitates critical inquiry into key questions of interest to vice principals and, at the same time, provides another means for professional growth in support of school and system goals and priorities. A study group of this nature provides vice principals with a collaborative, professionally supportive method of investigation and a means to augment their knowledge and skills. Because this learning team strategy involves a long-term commitment with direct classroom/school/system experimentation and ongoing dialogue among vice principals, the benefits to those involved—students, teachers, and other staff members within specific schools and across the system—is significant.

This team is an additional layer of support to that already being provided by the district and the Vice Principals' Association. Both experienced leaders and vice principals new to the position benefit from participation on the learning team. At a time when there is a shortage of experienced administrators, with a large number of vice principals new to the role and with little time for transition and training once the role is assumed, such a support group is especially helpful in developing the professional learning and leadership of all vice principals involved. Participants share school practices, issues, and resources, as well as participate in professional learning opportunities. The learning team sessions assist members in navigating leadership challenges, expanding leadership capabilities, and reflecting on best practices. Discussions also focus on decision-making skills and ways to motivate staff.

Meetings are held at the homes of vice principals or at a designated site. Each session begins with a social time from 5:00 PM to 6:00 PM, which includes dinner. The discussion from 6:00 PM to 8:00 PM focuses on a reading determined by the group. There is always a sharing component: what's working at my school; school issues; staff development attended; upcoming staff development opportunities; recommended reading.

Minutes are taken at each meeting. Agendas for each meeting as well as minutes from the previous meeting are circulated in advance. An annual report is submitted to the school district departments who funded the learning team.

The funding to support this learning team was sought and obtained from several departments of the school district. Some ideas on how to start a learning team at the district level and a sample proposal are provided below.

How to Start a Learning Team at the District Level

This is a formal format with accountability for the funding included. (An informal format would also be very valuable.)

- Gather a nucleus of school leaders who are interested in forming a learning team.
- Determine the purpose of the team—What do you want to learn?
- Decide on a format for meeting and develop a tentative budget for the year.
- Write and submit a proposal to district-level administrators who are in a position to support and fund the initiative.
- Upon approval, invite others of like mind to join the learning team.
- Use the initial meeting to finalize purposes and processes; establish meeting dates, locations, and rotating chairs; identify resources needed; and discuss professional development opportunities and goals.
- Record the agendas and minutes on an ongoing basis.
- Submit an annual report and request renewed funding.

Sample Proposal

Secondary Vice Principals Learning Team Proposal

Date:

To:

From:

Rationale

The learning team/circle model is a pedagogically proven format for professional learning; the collaborative, teacher-driven classroom inquiry process involved fosters partnership, teacher dialogue, and classroom transfer. Ongoing discussion about instructional issues has potential to improve instructional practice and student learning in meaningful ways.

A learning team of vice principals would facilitate critical inquiry into key questions of interest to vice principals and, at the same time, provide another means for professional growth in support of school and system goals and priorities. A study group of this nature would provide vice principals with a collaborative, professionally supportive method of investigation and a means to augment their knowledge and skills. Because this model involves a relatively long-term commitment with direct classroom/school/system experimentation and ongoing dialogue among vice principals, the benefits to those involved—students, teachers, and other staff members within specific schools and across the system—would be significant.

A learning team for secondary vice principals would be a layer of support in addition to that already being provided by the board and the Vice Principals' Association. Both experienced leaders and vice principals new to the position would benefit from participation on a learning team. At a time when there is a shortage of experienced administrators, with a large number of vice principals new to the role and with little time for transition and training once the role is assumed, such a support group would be especially helpful in developing the professional learning and leadership of all vice principals involved. Participants would share school practices, issues, and resources, as well as professional learning opportunities.

Benefits for Vice Principals Involved in Learning Team

- Vice principals are supported in terms of time and resources for professional learning.
- Vice principals are empowered to expand practices and to solve professional dilemmas in times of mandated changes to curriculum and operating procedures.
- Vice principals are provided with opportunities to deepen their knowledge and skills.
- Vice principals new to the role are given an opportunity to dialogue and develop a network of support in the presence of more experienced colleagues.

Benefits to Schools, Including Teachers and Students

- Implementation of school-based initiatives in keeping with district and school goals and priorities
- Professional growth of vice principals that mirrors and supports ongoing, in-school professional development
- Continued fostering of a culture of inquiry and reflection with positive impact on schools
- Students benefit from application of learning—an expected outcome of this project

Benefits to School District/System

- Ongoing, systemwide professional development
- Development of a system-based resource team

- Support for new and experienced vice principals interested in professional dialogue and inquiry

Process and Time Lines

Prior to June 200_, a study group of vice principals interested in pursuing an inquiry process of professional growth will be formed. This group will have specified resource needs and determined areas of investigation by the end of October 200_.

A summary of target dates includes the following:

- **Date:** _____—Information to vice principals (Monthly Association Meeting) and distribution of invitation
- **Date:** _____—Information session for potential participants to clarify membership purpose and establish possible areas of professional inquiry
- **Date:** _____—First meeting of learning team group to finalize purposes and processes; establish meeting dates, locations, and rotating chairs for 200_–200_ school year; identify resources needed; and discuss professional development opportunities and goals
- **Dates:** _____—Learning team continues to meet on a monthly basis.

Format of Meetings

Meetings would be held once a month at the homes of vice principals or a designated site. Each session would begin with a social time from 5:00 PM to 6:00 PM, which includes dinner. The discussion from 6:00 PM to 8:00 PM would focus on a reading determined by the group and would always include a sharing component (what's working at my school, school issues, staff development attended, upcoming staff development opportunities, recommended reading). These sessions will assist members to navigate leadership challenges, to expand leadership capabilities, and to reflect on best practices. Discussions would also focus on decision-making skills and ways to motivate staff. Minutes for each meeting would be taken. Agendas for each meeting, as well as minutes from the previous meeting, would be circulated in advance. An annual report would be submitted at the end of the school year.

Budget

Potential sources of funding include the following:

- Secondary Vice Principals' Association
- District Program Services
- District School Services
- Superintendent of Schools

Projected costs for 200_–200_ (based on a study group comprised of ___ vice-principals) are as follows:

Teachers on Administrative Duties (Coverage)	$****.00
(For visits to vice principal colleagues in other schools, staff development opportunities, in-school meetings)	
Professional Development Opportunities	$****.00
Books and Resources	$****.00
Refreshments	$****.00
(Ten meetings at members' homes with dinner included)	
Photocopying $ ***.00	

Total Projected Costs   **$****.00**

Thank you for your consideration of this learning opportunity for district vice principals.

The Principal's Toolkit

Reproducibles

Figure 1.1   The PLC Edifice

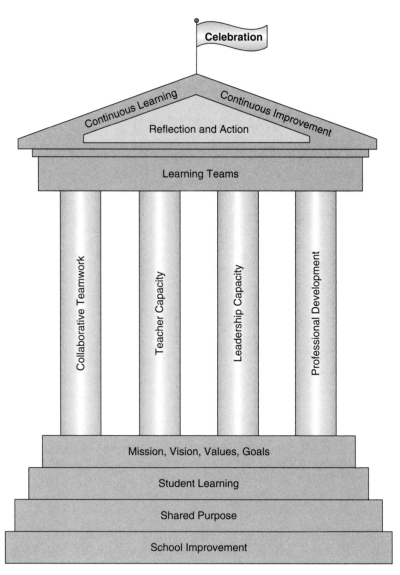

PLC Edifice

Reflection and Action Template

Core Practices of Successful Leaders*	**Reflection** *What practices are already in my leadership repertoire?*	**Action** *What practices will I act on as a PLC leader?*
Setting Directions		
Developing People		
Redesigning the Organization		
Managing the Instructional Program		

SOURCE: Leithwood et al., 2006.

Figure 3.1   PLC Snapshot Assessment

School: _____

Completed by: _____

Date: _____

Criteria	Stage 1 Knowledge	Stage 2 Application	Stage 3 Accomplishment	Reflection and Action
Shared Purpose of Student Learning				
Mission, Vision, Values, Goals				
Learning Teams				
Collaborative Teamwork				
Teacher Capacity				
Leadership Capacity				
Professional Development				
Continuous Learning and Improvement				
Reflection and Action				
Celebration				

PLC Learning Grid		
Knowledge/Key Ideas	*Strategy/Activity*	*Ways I Can Use . . .*

Figure 6.1   Reflection in Action Cycle

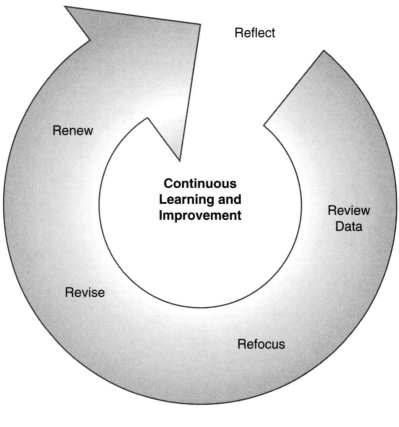

Reflection and Action

Figure PD1.1 Place Mat

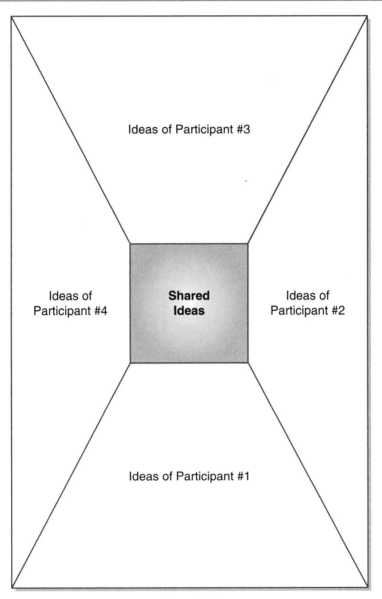

Place Mat

Figure PD1.3 Fishbone

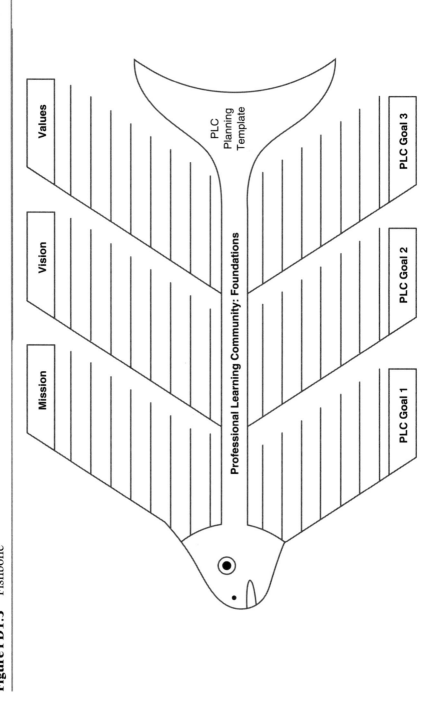

Values

Vision

Mission

PLC
Planning
Template

Professional Learning Community: Foundations

PLC Goal 1

PLC Goal 2

PLC Goal 3

Team Feedback Sheet

Team:	
Date:	
Team Members Present and Regrets:	
PLC Goal for Meeting:	
Next Steps:	
Team Responsibilities and Time Line:	
Administrator Review:	
Date:	

Glossary

Celebration: The positive recognition given to the accomplishments that result from collaborative action, especially those actions that contribute to improvement of student achievement. When principals and teachers learn together in a culture of respect, trust, and collective commitment to learning, their shared purpose is supported by many kinds of celebration.

Collaboration: The process by which all school staff work together within a framework of collective inquiry with the shared purpose of improving student achievement.

Collaborative teamwork: Teachers working together collaboratively in learning teams with their principals and other school staff to create a school culture where collective inquiry, reflective practice, and continuous professional development are used to design and implement effective instructional practices.

Continuous improvement: The ongoing cycle where learning teams focus on results constantly as they set goals, take action, review their results, and respond with new goals and further actions to support their own and their students' learning. This involves revising the school improvement plan, learning team plans, and individual teacher plans to improve student achievement results.

Continuous learning: A commitment to professional growth as a result of reflection on practice and the expectation that all teachers and leaders in the school should continue to build instructional capacity.

Fishbone: A graphic organizer in the shape of the spine of a fish, used in this book as a strategy for collaboratively developing mission, vision, values, and goals statements.

117

Goals: Planned actions that can be monitored and measured to assess progress toward the desired student achievement outcomes. In a PLC, goal setting is a very detailed and comprehensive activity requiring the school continually to reflect and assess how the goal statements support and promote the mission, vision, and values of the school.

Leadership capacity: The recognition that PLC principals continue to develop the core leadership practices of setting directions, building relationships, developing people, redesigning the organization, and managing the instructional program (Leithwood et al., 2006).

Learning team: A small group of professionals who agree to experiment with new ideas and meet regularly for a specific period of time to share specific professional growth experiences guided by specific goals and purposes. Learning team meetings are times for sharing lessons learned in the classroom and reflecting on the application of new knowledge and skills as it impacts student learning. Learning team meetings are structured to share successes and discuss strategies that worked in the classroom, as well as to share difficulties, to determine why they arose, and to find solutions.

Mission: Within the context of a PLC, a statement that clarifies what students will learn, how this learning will be assessed, and how educators will respond when students do not learn.

Place mat: A graphic organizer used by small groups to facilitate a think, pair, share experience by accessing prior knowledge and stimulating discussion.

PLC edifice: A graphic organizer that compares a PLC to a grand building, with the structural elements of a building corresponding to the attributes of a PLC.

PLC learning grid: A template that allows the reader to record significant ideas and strategies for the study and implementation of the attributes of a PLC, as well as consider ways in which this learning can be used in the school.

PLC portfolio: A tracking tool that provides a record of the school's accomplishments as it grows as a PLC. The PLC Portfolio presents the school as it is as it begins its journey into collaborative action for student learning and records the milestones as the PLC flourishes.

PLC snapshot assessment: A rubric that allows principals and their staffs to review their schools against a set of criteria that describes a PLC. This tool serves as both a diagnostic assessment and an ongoing check of progress in meeting the goal of establishing a PLC in the school.

PLC steering team: A collaborative leadership team of the principal and teacher representatives who share in decision making, planning, and implementation of the PLC in the school.

Professional development: Capacity building that includes both professional learning opportunities external to the school and the internal learning that occurs in collaborative teacher teams. PLCs make active use of job-embedded learning, where teachers develop their instructional practice through learning by doing in the classroom and having a process in place to assess collaboratively the results of their practice and respond to the data.

Professional development module: A detailed outline of a workshop presentation that school leaders can use to facilitate the introduction of the concept of a PLC to staff.

Professional learning community (PLC): A school environment where teachers work collaboratively in purposefully designed groups to improve student achievement within a structure of support provided by the school administrator. In such schools, principals create a culture where teachers work actively in teams with the shared purpose of producing successful learning outcomes for all students.

Reflection and action: A cycle of continuous improvement where results are reviewed reflectively, plans revised, and efforts refocused and renewed. This produces the synergy that supports action for improvement at all levels of the school.

School improvement: The school's continuing commitment to improve student achievement by supporting capacity building of teachers and leaders.

Shared purpose: A school culture where mission, vision, values, and goals are supportive of student learning through the application of the principles of a PLC.

SMART goals: An acronym that describes a goal-setting process where the goals are **S**pecific, **M**easurable, **A**ttainable, **R**esults oriented, and **T**ime bound (Conzemius & O'Neill, 2002).

Student learning: The commitment to improved student achievement, which is the most essential attribute of a PLC. It's not enough to ensure that students are taught. The issue is whether they learn. Teachers must ensure that students become ongoing learners with the knowledge, skills, and dispositions that make success possible (DuFour, Eaker, & DuFour, 2005).

Teacher capacity: A commitment to a strong professional culture where instructional practice is continually improving as teachers collaborate to initiate and assess effective instructional practice.

Values: A statement that presents the specific attitudes, behaviors, and commitments that principals and staff define as underlying their commitment to the mission and vision statements they have created.

Vision: The articulation of the image of the future that the school wants to build. In PLCs, vision is developed collaboratively and has the strength of reflecting the shared purpose of all educators in the school.

References

Barth, R. S. (2005). Turning book burners into lifelong learners. In R. DuFour, R. Eaker, & R. DuFour (Eds.), *On common ground: The power of professional learning communities* (pp. 115–134). Bloomington, IN: National Educational Service.

Blankstein, A. M. (2004). *Failure is NOT an option: Six principles that guide student achievement in high-performing schools.* Thousand Oaks, CA: Corwin Press and Hope Foundation.

Bolam, R., McMahon, A., Stoll, L., Thomas, S., & Wallace, M. (with Greenwood, A., Hawkey, K., Ingram, M., Atkinson, A., & Smith, M.). (2005). *Creating and sustaining effective professional learning communities* (Research Report RR637). England: Department for Education and Skills, University of Bristol. Available August 18, 2008, at http://www.dcsf.gov.uk/research/data/uploadfiles/RR637.pdf

Bredeson, P. V. (2003). *Designs for learning: A new architecture for professional development.* Thousand Oaks, CA: Corwin Press.

Conzemius, A., & O'Neill, J. (2002). *The handbook for SMART school teams.* Bloomington, IN: National Educational Service.

DuFour, R., DuFour, R., Eaker, R., & Karhanek, G. (2004). *Whatever it takes: How professional learning communities respond when kids don't learn.* Bloomington, IN: National Educational Service.

DuFour, R., & Eaker, R. (1998). *Professional learning communities at work: Best practices for enhancing student achievement.* Bloomington, IN: National Educational Service.

DuFour, R., Eaker, R., & DuFour, R. (Eds.). (2005). *On common ground: The power of professional learning communities.* Bloomington, IN: National Educational Service.

Eason-Watkins, B. (2005). Implementing PLCs in the Chicago public schools. In R. DuFour, R. Eaker, & R. DuFour (Eds.), *On common ground: The power of professional learning communities* (pp. 193–208). Bloomington, IN: National Educational Service.

Elmore, R. F. (2004). *School reform from the inside out: Policy, practice and performance.* Cambridge, MA: Harvard Education Press.

Fullan, M. (2001). *The new meaning of educational change* (3rd ed.). New York: Teachers College Press.

Fullan, M. (2005a). *Facilitator's guide: The moral imperative of school leadership.* Thousand Oaks, CA: Corwin Press.

Fullan, M. (2005b). *Leadership & sustainability: System thinkers in action.* Thousand Oaks, CA: Corwin Press.

Fullan, M. (2005c). Professional learning communities writ large. In R. DuFour, R. Eaker, & R. DuFour (Eds.), *On common ground: The power of professional learning communities* (pp. 209–223). New York: Teachers College Press.

Fullan, M. (2006). *Turnaround leadership.* San Francisco: Jossey-Bass.

Hargreaves, A. (2003). *Teaching in the knowledge society: Education in the age of insecurity.* New York: Teachers College Press.

Hargreaves, D. H. (2001). The knowledge-creating school. In B. Moon, J. Butcher, & E. Bird (Eds.), *Leading professional development in education* (pp. 224–240). London: RoutledgeFalmer.

Hord, S. M. (1997). *Professional learning communities: Communities of continuous inquiry and improvement* [Electronic version]. *SEDL Letter,* 6(1). Retrieved August 18, 2008, at the Southwest Educational Development Lab Web site: http://www.sedl.org/pubs/change34/

Hully, W., & Dier, L. (2005). *Harbours of hope: The planning for school and student success process.* Bloomington, IN: National Educational Service.

Leithwood, K., Day, C., Sammons, P., Harris, A., & Hopkins, D. (2006). *Successful school leadership: What it is and how it influences pupil learning* (Research Report RR800). England: Department for Education and Skills, University of Nottingham. Available August 18, 2008, at http://www.wallacefoundation.org

Leithwood, K., Seashore Louis, K., Anderson, S., & Wahlstrom, K. (2004). *How leadership influences student learning: A review of research.* New York: Wallace Foundation. Available August 18, 2008, at http://www.wallacefoundation.org

Lick, D. W. (2005, December 7). *Creating learning teams: The revolution begins with learning teams and learning communities.* Paper presented at the 2005 National Staff Development Council Conference, Philadelphia, PA.

National Staff Development Council (NSDC). (2001). *Standards for staff development* (rev. ed.). Oxford, OH: Author. Available August 18, 2008, at http://www.nsdc.org/standards/index.cfm

National Staff Development Council (NSDC). (2004). *Powerful designs for professional learning.* Oxford, OH: Author.

Sagor, R. (2004). *The action research guidebook: A four-step process for educators and school teams,* Thousand Oaks, CA: Corwin Press.

Schmoker, M. (2005). No turning back: The ironclad case for professional learning communities. In R. DuFour, R. Eaker, & R. DuFour (Eds.), *On common ground: The power of professional learning communities* (pp. 135–154). Bloomington, IN: National Educational Service.

Senge, P. (1990). *The fifth discipline: The art and practice of learning organization.* New York: Doubleday.

Senge, P. (2000). *Schools that learn: A fifth discipline fieldbook for educators, parents and everyone who cares.* New York: Doubleday.

Stiggins, R. (2005). Assessment FOR learning: Building a culture of confident learners. In R. DuFour, R. Eaker, & R. DuFour (Eds.), *On common ground: The power of professional learning communities* (pp. 65–84). Bloomington, IN: National Educational Service.

Stoll, L., & Seashore Louis, K. (2007). Professional learning communities: Elaborating new approaches. In L. Stoll & K. Seashore Louis (Eds.), *Professional learning communities* (pp. 1–14). Berkshire, England: Open University Press.

Index